THE WORLD OF BUSINESS

Student Workbook

Fifth Edition

John Pownall

Alyson Pownall

NELSON EDUCATION

NELSON EDUCATION

The World of Business
Student Workbook
Fifth Edition

Authors
John Pownall
Alyson Pownall

Vice President, School Division
Beverley Buxton

General Manager, Social Studies, Business Studies, and Languages
Carol Stokes

Publisher, Social Studies and Business Studies
Doug Panasis

Managing Editor, Development
Karin Fediw

Product Manager
Mary Jo Climie

Developmental Editor
Alisa Yampolsky

Editorial Assistant
Kimberly Murphy

Executive Director, Content and Media Production
Renate McCloy

Director, Content and Media Production
Lisa Dimson

Senior Content Production Manager
Sujata Singh

Junior Content Production Editor
Stephanie Erb

Copy Editor
Audrey Dorsch

Proofreader
Montgomery Kersell

Production Manager
Cathy Deak

Senior Production Coordinator
Kathrine Pummell

Design Director
Ken Phipps

Cover Design
Rocket Design

Cover Image
© 2008 JupiterImages and its Licensors. All Rights Reserved.

Compositor
Nelson Gonzalez

Permissions Researcher
Daniela Glass

Reviewers
The authors and publisher gratefully acknowledge the contributions of the following educators:

Kathleen Ryan Elliott
Kawartha Pine Ridge District
School Board, ON

Lorie Guest
Waterloo Region District School
Board, ON

David Notman
Limestone District School Board,
ON (retired)

Michelle Presotto
Toronto Catholic District School
Board, ON

Jack Wilson
Limestone District School Board,
ON (retired)

TABLE OF CONTENTS

UNIT 2: FUNCTIONS OF A BUSINESS

Chapter 5: Production

Chapter 6: Human Resources

Chapter 7: Management

Chapter 8: Marketing

CHAPTER 1: ECONOMIC BASICS

A. Business Vocabulary

In Chapter 1, you'll be introduced to some key business terms. Before you begin working with the chapter, browse through the pages and look for the bolded key terms. Use the left-hand side of the chart below to write any words you don't immediately understand. Then, when you arrive at the section featuring the word, write its definition in the middle column. Use the last column to note any relevant examples.

Term	Textbook Definition	Examples

B. Chapter Notes: What Is a Business?

Read the first section, What Is a Business? (pages 6–10), in your textbook, and use the following organizer to help guide your note-taking.

Seven characteristics can be used to classify a business. In the graphic organizer below, explain how each characteristic helps describe a business.

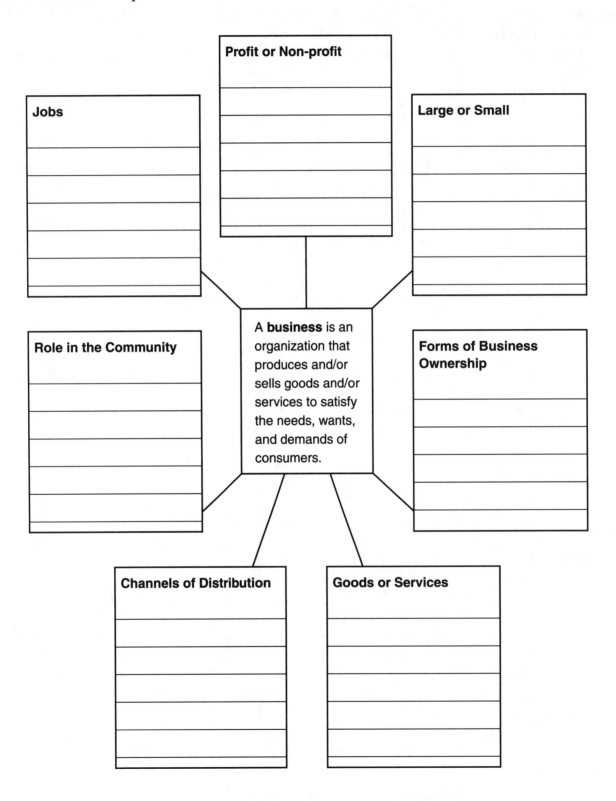

C. Activity: Profit or Non-profit?

One way to classify a business is by its primary motive for existence. For each business and organization listed, decide whether it is a for-profit or non-profit business/organization by placing an x in the appropriate column. Then describe its primary goal of operation.

Business/Organization	For-profit	Non-profit	Goal of Business/Organization
Daily Bread Food Bank			
YMCA			
Food Basics			
Chapters Indigo			
Habitat for Humanity			
Future Shop			
Value Village			
Canadian Breast Cancer Foundation			

D. Chapter Notes: The Role of the Consumer

Read the second section, The Role of the Consumer (pages 10–14), in your textbook, and answer the following questions.

1. What do the consuming habits of Canadians indicate to businesses? How do businesses use this information?

_____

_____

_____

_____

_____

2. Explain how competition among businesses can influence a marketplace.

_____

_____

_____

_____

_____

3. Why might a product become obsolete? Provide two examples.

_____

_____

_____

_____

4. When determining the price of a product, what factors must producers take into account? What is the effect of such a decision?

_____

_____

_____

_____

5. Explain the difference between a customer and consumer.

_____

_____

_____

_____

E. Activity: Consumer Influence

Over time, a shift has occurred from businesses controlling the marketplace to consumers having more influence on decisions that are made in the marketplace.

For each item listed below, provide an example of how consumers have influenced the product, price, or service. The first row has been completed as an example.

Item	How have consumers influenced this product?
Cars	More variety in types of vehicles available as consumers are looking for different sizes of cars depending on their lifestyles (e.g., minivans vs. sports cars) and the development of new features (e.g., global positioning systems [GPS], seat warmers, MP3 players).
Jeans	
Cereal	
Pop	
Fast food	
Cellphones	
Event tickets	

F. Activity: Obsolescence

A product that has become obsolete has experienced a decline in its value brought about by an introduction of new technology or changes in demand. As technology changes, new products replace existing ones. This process is ongoing.

1. Each product listed below is in danger of becoming obsolete in the next 10 years. For each one, list the new product(s) that may replace it and explain the ways in which the new product is superior.

Product	What new products may cause it to become obsolete?	In what ways is the new product superior?
Floppy disks		
Film camera		
Portable CD player		
Gift certificates		
Videotapes		

2. Explain why a product might fail in one market but survive in another. Provide an example.

_____

_____

_____

_____

_____

3. List three products in current use that you believe will never become obsolete. What will give these products staying power?

_____

_____

_____

_____

G. Chapter Notes: Starting a Business

Read the third section, Starting a Business (pages 15–22), in your textbook, and answer the following questions.

1. List four characteristics required of an entrepreneur.

   _____

   _____

   _____

   _____

2. When planning a new business, what factors need to be considered with respect to potential consumers?

   _____

   _____

   _____

   _____

   _____

3. There are three ways a business can respond to customer feedback:

   1. _____

   2. _____

   3. _____

4. Explain how having too much inventory can hinder a business.

   _____

   _____

   _____

   _____

5. List the five steps of the decision-making model.

   Step 1: _____

   Step 2: _____

   Step 3: _____

   Step 4: _____

   Step 5: _____

H. Activity: Needs and Wants

Needs have been defined as goods or services that are required for survival. This includes the need for food, clothing, shelter, and health care, as well as the means to secure them. Wants are goods or services that arc not necessary but are desired. You need clothes, but you do not need designer clothes.

1. Complete the checklist below, indicating whether the product is a need, a want, or both. Explain your selection.

Product	Need	Want	Explanation
Cellphone			
Concert tickets			
Medication to control high blood pressure			
Plumbing tools for a plumber			
Vehicle to attend school			
Bag of chips			

2. Discuss the following situations with a partner and record your responses in the space provided.

a) How does Christmastime shopping illustrate consumer spending on wants?

_____

_____

_____

_____

_____

_____

_____

_____

_____

b) Explain how a want for one person can be a need for another. Provide an example.

_____

_____

_____

_____

_____

_____

_____

_____

_____

_____

c) In the 1920s, cars were a luxury good. Now many people feel that a car is a need. What factors can cause a good to evolve from a want to a need? Provide an example.

_____

_____

_____

_____

_____

_____

_____

_____

_____

_____

I. Activity: Decision-Making Model

Making decisions and solving problems are things that you do several times a day. For most minor decisions, such as deciding what to wear in the morning, a structured decision-making process is not necessary. Though you may not use a formal decision-making process often, in complex situations, it can help you avoid serious negative consequences. Becoming a good decision maker means you are fully aware of your options.

1. Take a problem of your choice and apply the five-step decision-making model to it.

Step 1—Determine what decision has to be made.	
Step 2—Identify the alternatives.	
Step 3—Evaluate the advantages and disadvantages of each alternative.	
Step 4—Make a decision and take action.	
Step 5—Evaluate the decision.	

2. A decision matrix can also help you make a decision. Down the first column, list all of the possible decision alternatives. Enter the criteria for your decision along the top. Use a separate sheet to add more criteria and more alternatives if necessary. Assign a weight to each factor, using a numerical value from 1 to 10. For a negative factor such as risk, a high number would indicate low risk. The best choice is the one with the highest number when you total each row. See the model below for an example. Use the blank decision matrix to evaluate the alternatives for your decision from activity #1. Is the outcome the same?

Example:

Decision to be made: *What Business courses should I take in Grade 11?*

	College Prep Available	Real-Life Relatability	Interest in Subject Matter	Total
Marketing	Yes – 7	8	9	24
Entrepreneurship	Yes – 7	6	6	19
Information and Communication Technology	No – 3	8	7	18

Decision to be made:

	Criteria 1	Criteria 2	Criteria 3	Total
Choice 1				
Choice 2				
Choice 3				

J. Chapter Notes: Economic Resources

Read the fourth section, Economic Resources (pages 22–28), in your textbook, and use the following organizer to help guide your note-taking. Then answer the question that follows.

1. Define each type of economic resource, and provide several examples.

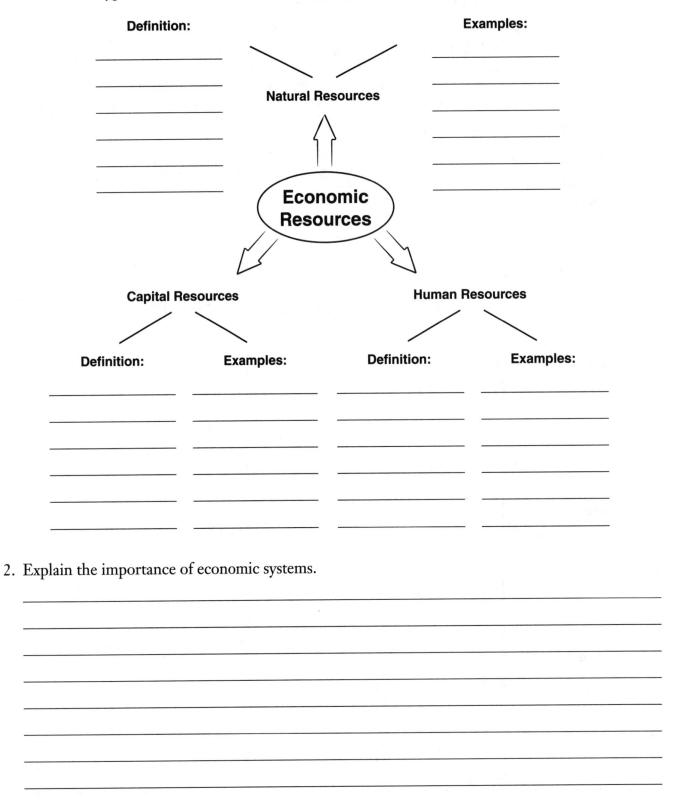

Definition:

_____
_____
_____
_____
_____
_____

Examples:

_____
_____
_____
_____
_____

Natural Resources

Economic Resources

Capital Resources

Human Resources

Definition:

_____
_____
_____
_____
_____
_____

Examples:

_____
_____
_____
_____
_____
_____

Definition:

_____
_____
_____
_____
_____
_____

Examples:

_____
_____
_____
_____
_____
_____

2. Explain the importance of economic systems.

_____
_____
_____
_____
_____
_____
_____
_____
_____

K. Activity: Comparing Economic Systems

The World Factbook, put together by the United States Central Intelligence Agency (CIA), is an excellent source of information about every country. Examine the data in the table below and answer the questions that follow.

(Data in the CIA *World Factbook* is updated throughout the year. This was the data on April 27, 2007.)

	Canada	Romania	Jamaica
Total population	33 390 141	22 276 056	2 780 132
Gross domestic product per capita	$35 200	$8800	$4600
Labour force	17 590 000	9 330 000	1 100 000
% of population working in agriculture	2%	31.6%	18.1%
% of population working in industry	14%	30.7%	17.3%
% of population working in services	75%	37.7%	64.6%
% of population living below the poverty line	15.9%	25%	14.8%
Exports— commodities	Motor vehicles and parts, industrial machinery, aircraft, telecommunications equipment, chemicals, plastics, fertilizers, wood pulp, timber, crude petroleum, natural gas, electricity, aluminum.	Textiles and footwear, metals and metal products, machinery and equipment, minerals and fuels, chemicals, agricultural products.	Alumina, bauxite, sugar, bananas, rum, coffee, yams, beverages, chemicals, wearing apparel, mineral fuels.
Exports (in $)	$405 billion	$33 billion	$2.087 billion
Export partners by %	U.S.A. 84.2%, Japan 2.1%, U.K. 1.8%	Italy 19.4%, Germany 14%, Turkey 7.9%, France 7.4%, U.K. 5.5%, Hungary 4.1%, U.S.A. 4.1%	U.S.A. 25.8%, Canada 19.3%, U.K. 10.7%, Netherlands 8.6%, China 7%, Norway 6.4%, Germany 5.6%
Imports— commodities	Machinery and equipment, motor vehicles and parts, crude oil, chemicals, electricity, durable consumer goods.	Machinery and equipment, fuels and minerals, chemicals, textiles and products, basic metals, agricultural products.	Food and other consumer goods, industrial supplies, fuel, parts and accessories of capital goods, machinery and transport equipment, construction materials.
Imports (in $)	$353.2 billion	$46.48 billion	$4.682 billion
Import partners by %	U.S.A. 56.7%, China 7.8%, Mexico 3.8%	Italy 15.5%, Germany 14%, Russia 8.3%, France 6.8%, Turkey 4.9%, China 4.1%	U.S.A. 41.4%, Trinidad and Tobago 14%, Venezuela 5.5%, Japan 4.6%

1. What percentage of the population of each country is in the labour force?

_____

_____

2. What are the similarities and differences between the three countries in terms of the percentage of the population that works in each type of industry?

_____

_____

_____

_____

_____

_____

3. Why might the list of Canadian exports be so much longer than that of Romania?

_____

_____

_____

_____

_____

4. Why might some commodities appear on both a country's import and export list? Provide an example to explain your answer.

_____

_____

_____

_____

_____

_____

5. Exports and imports total in the billions of dollars for each country. Explain what this tells you about our society.

_____

_____

_____

_____

_____

_____

L. Chapter Notes: Demand, Supply, and Price

Read the fifth section, Demand, Supply, and Price (pages 28–32), in your textbook, and answer the following questions.

1. Explain the law of demand.

   _____

2. What conditions create demand?

   _____

   _____

   _____

3. Briefly explain the four factors that increase or decrease demand.

   _____

   _____

   _____

   _____

   _____

   _____

4. Explain the law of supply.

   _____

5. What conditions affect supply?

   _____

   _____

6. Briefly explain the five factors that can increase or decrease supply.

   _____

   _____

   _____

   _____

   _____

7. Explain the relationship of price to supply and demand.

   _____

   _____

M. Activity: Supply and Demand

The relationship between supply and demand is a fundamental concept of economics and forms the basis of our economy. Product prices are a reflection of supply and demand. Keep this in mind as you read each statement below. Indicate whether the statement is true or false by placing an x in the appropriate column.

Statement	True	False	Explanation
If supply is high, prices will go down.			
Competition keeps prices high.			
Consumer decisions do not affect the economy.			
Knowing demand helps a business to decide how much of a good to produce.			
If demand is high, prices will go down.			
Unemployment affects demand.			
Lower production costs decrease profits.			

N. Activity: Changing Prices

Have you noticed prices changing? What was the reason for the increase or decrease in price? What role did supply, demand, and competition play? In the first column, list 10 examples of goods or services that have had a price change. In the second column, indicate whether the price increased or decreased. Determine the reason for the price change and indicate your answer using columns three, four, and/or five (e.g., more supply, less demand, more competition). The first row has been filled in for you as an example.

Good/Service	Increase/ Decrease in Price	Supply	Demand	Competition
Oranges	increase	less supply	n/a	n/a

O. Case Study: Megan and Danielle's Clothing Business

Megan and Danielle have been friends since high school Business class and are thinking of starting a small, upscale clothing store for young professional women. They would like to sell clothes, accessories, shoes, and Danielle's custom-made handbags. Their potential target market would be professional females, aged 25 to 35. They both feel that the time is right to start their own independent business after a decade of working for other people. Although they are excited to start their business, they have been struggling with how to determine the price at which to sell their goods and how to attract customers to their new store. They are hoping to keep costs as low as possible as they do not have a lot of capital to spend on advertising or market research.

1. What are the two issues that Megan and Danielle are struggling with?

_____

_____

_____

_____

_____

2. Discuss at least two ways they can determine the prices for their products.

_____

_____

_____

_____

_____

3. How can Megan and Danielle attract new customers to their store?

_____

_____

_____

_____

_____

_____

4. What may happen if there is a large demand for Danielle's custom-made handbags and not enough supply?

_____

_____

_____

Business Word Bank		
capital resources	goods	non-profit organization
consumer purchasing power	human resources	obsolete
consumers	interdependent	pricing power
costs	inventory	producer
demand	law of demand	profit
economic system	law of supply	services
entrepreneur	marketplace	solvency
expenses	natural resources	supply
factors of production	needs	wants

Use the terms given in the word bank to complete the following statements:

1. _____ is the income that is left after all costs and expenses are paid.

2. Wages are an example of _____ that are involved in running a business.

3. _____ are the amounts of money needed for each stage of production.

4. The ability of a business to pay all of its debts is known as _____.

5. A(n) _____ raises money to support a specific goal.

6. A business can be classified by the _____ it produces or the _____ it offers.

7. An example of a(n) _____ is a business that manufactures DVDs; _____ are the people who buy the DVDs.

8. A(n) _____ is any location where buyers and sellers come together to engage in the buying and selling of goods and services.

9. Portable cassette players have become _____ and have been replaced by portable CD and MP3 players.

10. When businesses have control over the marketplace, they have _____ and can charge high prices and raise prices when costs go up.

11. Consumers' ability to choose where they will buy goods and services and how much they will pay for them is known as _____.

12. A person who takes advantage of an opportunity and starts a business is a(n) _____.

13. Businesses attempt to meet either consumer _____ for items necessary for survival or _____ for things that add convenience and comfort to life.

14. _____ is the quantity of goods kept on hand by a business.

15. A combination of economic resources or _____ makes goods and services available to consumers.

16. Iron ore, fish, trees, and crude oil are examples of _____.

17. _____ are the people who work to create goods and services.

18. Trucks, machinery, and the money to buy raw materials and services are examples of _____.

19. A(n) _____ considers how goods and services will be produced, distributed, and consumed.

20. Our society is _____, which means that it relies on the goods and services provided by thousands of different businesses to satisfy consumer needs and wants.

21. The quantity of a good or service that consumers are willing and able to buy at a given price is known as _____. _____ is the quantity of a good or service that businesses are willing to provide within the price range that people are willing to pay.

22. According to the _____, when a product is desired by a large number of consumers but the quantity is limited, its price will tend to rise.

23. The relationship of increasing the quantity supplied as prices increase is called the _____.

CHAPTER 2: TYPES OF BUSINESSES

A. Business Vocabulary

In Chapter 2, you'll encounter some terms that describe different types of businesses. Before you begin working with the chapter, browse through the pages and look for the bolded key terms. Use the left-hand side of the chart below to write any words you don't immediately understand. Then, when you arrive at the section featuring the word, write its definition in the middle column. Use the last column to note any relevant examples.

Term	Textbook Definition	Examples

B. Chapter Notes: Forms of Business Ownership

Read the first section, Forms of Business Ownership (pages 41–49), in your textbook, and use the following organizer to help guide your note-taking.

Briefly describe the advantages and disadvantages of each type of business.

Type of Business	Advantages	Disadvantages
Sole proprietorship		
Partnership		
Corporation		
Co-operative		
Franchise		

C. Activity: Characteristics of Business Ownership

Listed below are some characteristics of the way businesses are organized or conduct their affairs. For each characteristic, determine the type of business it applies to and put an x in the appropriate column. NOTE: Some characteristics may relate to more than one type of business.

Characteristic	Sole Proprietorship	Partnership	Corporation	Co-operative	Franchise
Owner receives all of the profits and is responsible for all debts.					
Operated by two or more people who share costs and responsibilities.					
The easiest type of business to start and administer.					
Managed by a board of directors.					
Parent company often advertises on behalf of all of its operators.					
One vote per share.					
One vote per owner regardless of the number of shares owned.					
Primary motive is service, not profit.					
Operator pays a monthly fee to the parent company.					
Owned by members who buy products or use services offered by the business.					
Liability can be limited or unlimited, depending on the agreement.					

Your cousin Rohan has been thinking about owning a franchise but isn't sure if it's the right decision for him. He knows that you are currently taking a Business class and is hoping you could provide him with some more information. Using the information found on pages 47 to 49, write Rohan an e-mail outlining the nature of franchise ownership and explaining its benefits and drawbacks. Be sure to include some examples of franchises he may be interested in pursuing.

Hey, Rohan,

_____

_____

_____

_____

_____

_____

_____

_____

_____

_____

_____

_____

_____

_____

_____

_____

_____

_____

_____

_____

_____

_____

_____

_____

_____

E. Chapter Notes: Going into Business

Read the second section, Going into Business (pages 50–61), in your textbook, and answer the following questions.

1. Create a list of reasons why someone would want to start a business.

   _____

   _____

2. Describe the four types of businesses and provide an example for each.

   _____

   _____

   _____

   _____

   _____

   _____

3. How has technology influenced home-based businesses?

   _____

   _____

   _____

   _____

   _____

4. List three reasons why consumers may be hesitant about shopping online.

   _____

   _____

   _____

   _____

5. Explain the disadvantages of debt financing and equity financing.

   _____

   _____

   _____

6. Outline five steps you need to take before starting your own business.

   _____

   _____

   _____

   _____

F. Activity: Risky Business

Starting and operating a business can be a risky undertaking, even if you've done preliminary research and planning. The task of any new business owner is to minimize potential risk by taking precautions. When situations come up, owners have to react quickly to reduce or eliminate these risks.

For each situation listed below, comment on how you would respond to help solve the problem and minimize the risk for the business.

1. One of your business's customers is not satisfied with your work and wants a full refund.

   _____

   _____

   _____

   _____

2. One of your investors decides to pull out at the last minute.

   _____

   _____

   _____

   _____

3. One of your business's biggest customers notifies you that they are going out of business, but they still owe your business a great deal of money.

   _____

   _____

   _____

   _____

4. Your business partner, Leigh, decided to buy new equipment for your business without consulting you.

   _____

   _____

   _____

   _____

5. One of your sales representatives is rude to a customer, and that customer is threatening to pull out of a deal with you.

   _____

   _____

   _____

   _____

G. Chapter Notes: International Business Structures

Read the third section, International Business Structures (pages 62–68), in your textbook, and use the following organizer to help guide your note-taking.

Briefly describe each type of international business structure and provide an example of each.

International Business Structure	Definition	Benefits to Business	Examples
Joint venture			
International franchise			
Strategic alliance			

International Business Structure	Definition	Benefits to Business	Examples
Merger			
Offshoring			
Multinational corporation			

H. Activity: Strategic Alliances

The term *strategic alliance* is used to describe an agreement between businesses to commit resources to achieve a common set of objectives.

1. For each example below, explain how each business benefits from a strategic alliance with the other.

   Amazon/HMV

   _____

   _____

   _____

   _____

   MSN.ca/CTV News

   _____

   _____

   _____

   _____

   Visa/Wal-Mart

   _____

   _____

   _____

   _____

   Scotiabank/Cineplex—Scene Program

   _____

   _____

   _____

   _____

2. Find more examples of businesses that have a strategic alliance.

   _____

   _____

   _____

   _____

   _____

I. Case Study: Detailed Design Drafting Services Ltd.

Located on Vancouver Island, Detailed Design Drafting Services Ltd. is a medium-sized company that adapts sets of engineering drawings into fabrication drawings, which are subsequently sent to a fabrication shop for construction. Owner and president Nick Osmond founded the company in 1997. In its first year, it operated as a traditional business and achieved modest growth. In 1998, it launched a website and was repositioned as an e-commerce operation. The company now employs a skilled team of engineers, project managers, information technology technicians, and senior, intermediate, and junior detailers.

The company's original market was the surrounding area of Vancouver Island and the Greater Vancouver Mainland Region. Since it developed e-commerce capability, its markets have shifted entirely to the United States. One hundred percent of its current sales are to American fabricators, of which 80 percent are medium-sized and 20 percent are large companies. Detailed Design Drafting Services Ltd. conducts business in 12 states, with the heaviest concentration in New York State and Utah. Recently, the company entered into a key supplier relationship with a company in Shanghai, China, to whom it intends to subcontract 10 percent of its detailing volume to increase its profitability and support market demand for the company's services. Osmond claims that this Shanghai company can deliver much of the required detailing through the Internet at one-fifth of his production cost.

1. Why would Detailed Design Drafting Services Ltd. consider subcontracting business to China? Identify a potential disadvantage of this strategy.

   _____

   _____

   _____

   _____

2. How has e-commerce changed the marketplace for Detailed Design Drafting Services Ltd.?

   _____

   _____

   _____

   _____

3. With a partner, develop a list of five other businesses that could use e-commerce to expand into new markets.

   _____

   _____

   _____

   _____

   _____

J. Review

Business Word Bank		
board of directors	general partnership	private corporation
co-operative	joint venture	public corporation
crown corporation	limited liability	revenue
debt financing	limited partnership	share
dividend	merger	shareholders
e-commerce	multinational corporations	SOHO
equity financing	offshoring	sole proprietorship
forecasting	partnership	strategic alliance
franchisee	partnership agreement	unlimited liability
franchiser		

Use the terms given in the word bank to complete the following statements:

1. A(n) _____ is a business owned by a single person.

2. The biggest disadvantage of sole proprietorship is that the proprietor has _____ and is fully responsible for all of the losses of the business.

3. The sharing of costs and responsibilities between two or more owners is considered a(n) _____.

4. A(n) _____ outlines the terms of a partnership. In a(n) _____, all partners have unlimited liability for the firm's debts. In a(n) _____, on the other hand, each partner's liability is limited to the amount of his or her investment.

5. With _____, owners' responsibility for business debts is restricted to the amount invested.

6. A unit of ownership in a corporation is called a(n) _____.

7. A(n) _____ is put into place to manage the money of _____.

8. Shareholders may receive a share of a company's profits in the form of a(n) _____.

9. A corporation owned by a small number of owners is considered a(n) _____, while a corporation with many shareholders is known as a(n) _____.

10. A business operated by the federal or provincial government is a(n) _____.

11. A business owned by the workers or members who buy the goods or services of the business is a(n) _____.

12. Subway is an example of a(n) _____ that licenses the rights to use its name to another business, the _____.

13. Home-based businesses are sometimes referred to as _____.

14. _____ allows shoppers to use the Internet to buy goods at home.

15. Getting a bank loan to start your business is an example of _____. Starting a business using investors' money is an example of _____.

16. _____ allows businesses to predict future conditions.

17. Subtracting costs and expenses from _____ determines whether a business has turned a profit or a loss.

18. A(n) _____ combines the skills and expertise of two different businesses so that both benefit.

19. The alliance between CBC and the *Toronto Star* is an example of a(n) _____.

20. A(n) _____ occurs when two or more companies join together to become a single organization.

21. A Canadian company that moves its manufacturing to China is practising _____.

22. _____ take advantage of the best resources of several countries.

CHAPTER 3: BUSINESS ETHICS AND SOCIAL RESPONSIBILITY

A. Business Vocabulary

In Chapter 3, you'll encounter some terms that have to do with ethical behaviour in business. Before you begin working with the chapter, browse through the pages and look for the bolded key terms. Use the left-hand side of the chart below to write any words you don't immediately understand. Then, when you arrive at the section featuring the word, write its definition in the middle column. Use the last column to note any relevant examples.

Term	Textbook Definition	Examples

Read the first section, Business Ethics (pages 75–89), in your textbook, and answer the following questions.

1. Define ethical behaviour. Why is it important in our society?

   _____

   _____

   _____

   _____

   _____

   _____

2. Why might a conflict between morals and values make a decision difficult?

   _____

   _____

   _____

   _____

   _____

   _____

3. What is a code of ethics? Why do businesses implement codes of ethics?

   _____

   _____

   _____

   _____

   _____

   _____

4. What factors are in conflict when a business faces an ethical dilemma? Name five ethical dilemmas a business may face.

   _____

   _____

   _____

   _____

   _____

   _____

5. When faced with an ethical dilemma, what factors should a person take into account before making a decision?

_____

_____

_____

_____

_____

6. On what type of issues does whistle-blowing tend to occur? Give two examples.

_____

_____

_____

_____

_____

7. Explain three types of fraud.

_____

_____

_____

_____

_____

8. Explain the importance of auditors in public companies.

_____

_____

_____

_____

_____

9. Explain why insider trading is both unethical and illegal.

_____

_____

_____

_____

_____

C. Activity: Ethical or Unethical?

Solving ethical dilemmas can be difficult for both businesses and individuals. To make the decision, it helps to ask yourself several questions. For each situation given, consider your answer to each of the questions and then make a decision.

1. Your boss tells you to shred documents pertaining to a lawsuit against the company. Do you do it?

   a) Who will be helped if you do it? _____

   b) Who will be hurt if you do it? _____

   c) What are the benefits of doing it? _____

   _____

   d) What are the problems of doing it? _____

   _____

   e) Will the action stand the test of time? _____

   _____

   Your decision: _____

   _____

2. A boy/girl that your best friend has a crush on asks you out on a date. Do you agree?

   a) Who will be helped if you agree? _____

   b) Who will be hurt if you agree? _____

   c) What are the benefits of agreeing? _____

   _____

   d) What are the problems of agreeing? _____

   _____

   e) Will the action stand the test of time? _____

   _____

   Your decision: _____

   _____

3. You see someone getting bullied at school, and he yells out for your help. Do you help him out?

   a) Who will be helped if you help him out? _____

   b) Who will be hurt if you help him out? _____

   c) What are the benefits of helping him out? _____

   _____

d) What are the problems of helping him out? _____

_____

e) Will the action stand the test of time? _____

_____

Your decision: _____

_____

4. A classmate offers you the answers to an upcoming exam. Do you take them?

a) Who will be helped if you take them? _____

b) Who will be hurt if you take them? _____

c) What are the benefits of taking them? _____

_____

d) What are the problems of taking them? _____

_____

e) Will the action stand the test of time? _____

_____

Your decision: _____

_____

5. You catch a needy friend shoplifting food for her family. Do you report her?

a) Who will be helped if you don't report her? _____

b) Who will be hurt if you don't report her? _____

c) What are the benefits of not reporting her? _____

_____

d) What are the problems of not reporting her? _____

_____

e) Will the action stand the test of time? _____

_____

Your decision: _____

_____

D. Activity: Evaluating (Un)ethical Behaviour

For each case below, explain whether the behaviour was ethical or unethical, and explain why.

1. Some Ontario lottery retailers have been accused of claiming the winnings of their patrons for themselves.

   _____

   _____

   _____

   _____

2. Menu Foods, a manufacturer of pet foods, recalled a large amount of its products because of concerns that the food was tainted and harmful to animals.

   _____

   _____

   _____

   _____

3. A teenager in the United States bought a large number of shares in a penny stock and, through postings on stock-tip websites, convinced other investors that the stock was the next big winner. As investors purchased the stock, the price per share went up. The teenager then sold his large number of shares at the inflated price and left the other investors with shares that were worth significantly less than what they had paid for them.

   _____

   _____

   _____

4. The Public Utilities Commission was aware of E. coli contamination in the drinking water of Walkerton, Ontario, days before it informed the public.

   _____

   _____

   _____

5. Consumer Reports, an independent product tester, informed the public that a report published about the safety of infant car seats had been flawed.

   _____

   _____

   _____

   _____

E. Activity: Ethics and Business

The following scrambled words can be found in Chapter 3 of *The World of Business*. Unscramble each of the words and write it in the space provided. Use the numbers below the words to find the mystery word at the bottom of the page.

ARFUD

_ _ _ _ _
    1

OAECGLINCN OIFTMNORINA

_ _ _ _ _ _ _ _ _   _ _ _ _ _ _ _ _ _ _
   2   4

MBENTEZLZEME

_ _ _ _ _ _ _ _ _ _ _
3   10

EHTFT

_ _ _ _ _
  5

IUSSEM FO NFDUS

_ _ _ _ _ _ _ _ _ _ _ _
  6   17

ERTMGAIPN HWTI ERODRSC

_ _ _ _ _ _ _ _ _ _ _ _ _ _ _ _ _ _ _
  8   15   11

NRINIIOTDSIMCA

_ _ _ _ _ _ _ _ _ _ _ _ _
    7

RFOGYER

_ _ _ _ _ _ _
  18

RONTEENALIMVN ISOINAVLTO

_ _ _ _ _ _ _ _ _ _ _ _ _
                         9

_ _ _ _ _ _ _ _ _ _ _
14   13

MYRPLOEE FTEHT

_ _ _ _ _ _ _ _ _ _ _ _ _
      16   12

_ _ _ _ _ _ _ _ _ _ _ _ _ _ _ _ _ _
1 2 3 4 5 6 7 8 9 10 11 12 13 14 15 16 17 18

F. Chapter Notes: Ethics and Corporate Social Responsibility

Read the second section, Ethics and Corporate Social Responsibility (pages 90–105), in your textbook, and answer the following questions.

1. Define the characteristics associated with socially responsible businesses.

   _____

   _____

   _____

   _____

2. Explain the benefits of each of the six corporate social responsibility (CSR) principles.

   1. _____

   _____

   2. _____

   _____

   3. _____

   _____

   4. _____

   _____

   5. _____

   _____

   6. _____

   _____

3. Explain the concept of duty to report.

   _____

   _____

   _____

   _____

4. How has Ontario's *Occupational Health and Safety Act* (OHSA) helped make workplace safety a priority for employers?

   _____

   _____

   _____

   _____

5. Who is most likely to face a glass ceiling in the workplace?

_____

_____

_____

_____

6. Define harassment and provide three examples.

_____

_____

_____

_____

7. Explain the concept of duty to accommodate.

_____

_____

_____

_____

8. Explain why businesses have been slow to implement environmentally friendly strategies.

_____

_____

_____

_____

9. List five highlights of the *Canadian Environmental Protection Act* (CEPA).

Highlights of the act include

1. _____

2. _____

3. _____

4. _____

5. _____

10. What is the Kyoto Protocol? Why has it been difficult to implement?

_____

_____

_____

_____

11. Explain how addressing environmental concerns can increase a business's profits.

_____

_____

_____

_____

_____

12. What is the *Employment Standards Act*?

_____

_____

_____

_____

_____

13. Compared to men, how much do full-time women workers earn? What are some possible explanations for the gap in pay between men and women?

_____

_____

_____

_____

_____

14. What is the *Personal Information Protection and Electronic Documents Act*?

_____

_____

_____

_____

_____

15. Explain how fair trade is an example of ethical trading.

_____

_____

_____

_____

_____

G. Activity: Top 10 Reasons for Business Ethics

1. Imagine that you run a business. Using the top-10 list on page 92 of your textbook, rank your top 10 reasons for having an ethical business according to your personal views of ethical behaviour.

   1. _____
   2. _____
   3. _____
   4. _____
   5. _____
   6. _____
   7. _____
   8. _____
   9. _____
   10. _____

2. What did you rank as your top reason? Why?

   _____
   _____
   _____
   _____
   _____
   _____
   _____
   _____
   _____
   _____

3. What reason ranked last? Why?

   _____
   _____
   _____
   _____
   _____
   _____
   _____
   _____
   _____
   _____

H. Activity: Corporate Ethics

For each action listed in the first column, place an x in the appropriate box to indicate the area(s) of law it falls under. NOTE: For some actions, more than one area of law may apply.

Action	Health and Safety	Anti-discrimination	Harassment	Accessibility	Environmental Responsibility	Labour Practices
Telling racist jokes						
Building a ramp for wheelchair-bound employees						
Allowing employees to work flexible hours						
Establishing waste reduction programs						
Not hiring someone because of a physical disability						
Paying a woman less than a man to do work of a similar nature						
Encouraging others to insult someone based on race						
Defining workers' rights and responsibilities						
Dumping toxic waste in the lake						

I. Activity: Fair Trade

Use the space provided to write a letter to your school board, asking that it mandate the use of fair-trade products in the cafeteria. Your letter should define fair trade and provide some examples. Be sure to explain the ethical problem of not using fair trade and why it is an important global issue that needs to be addressed. NOTE: You may wish to use pages 103 to 105 of your textbook for reference.

Dear Board Members:

_____

_____

_____

_____

_____

_____

_____

_____

_____

_____

_____

_____

_____

_____

_____

_____

_____

_____

_____

_____

_____

_____

_____

_____

J. Case Study: Whistle-Blowing and the Environment

Chantale Leroux works as a clerk for Avco Environmental Services, a small toxic-waste disposal company. The company has a contract to dispose of medical waste from a local hospital. During the course of her work, Chantale comes across documents that suggest Avco has actually been disposing of some of this medical waste in a local municipal landfill. Chantale is shocked. She knows this practice is illegal. And even though only a small portion of the medical waste that Avco handles is disposed of this way, any amount at all seems a worrisome threat to public health.

Chantale gathers the appropriate documents and takes them to her immediate superior, Dave Lamb. Dave says, "Look, I don't think that sort of thing is your concern, or mine. We're in charge of record keeping, not making decisions about where this stuff gets dumped. I suggest you drop it."

The next day, Chantale decides to go one step further and talk to Angela van Wilgenburg, the company's operations manager. Angela is clearly irritated. Angela says, "This isn't your concern. Look, these are the sorts of cost-cutting moves that let a little company like ours compete with our giant competitors. Besides, everyone knows that the regulations in this area are overly cautious. There's no real danger to anyone from the tiny amount of medical waste that 'slips' into the municipal dump. I consider this matter closed."

Chantale considers her situation. The message from her superiors was loud and clear. She strongly suspects that making further noises about this issue could jeopardize her job. Further, she generally has faith in the company's management. They've always seemed like honest, trustworthy people. But she is troubled by this apparent disregard for public safety. On the other hand, she asks herself whether maybe Angela is right in arguing that the danger is minimal. Chantale looks up the phone number of an old friend who worked for the local newspaper.

1. What ethical dilemma is Chantale facing?

_____

_____

_____

_____

2. Is Avco Environmental demonstrating socially responsible behaviour? Why or why not?

_____

_____

_____

3. What do you think Chantale should do? Explain your reasoning.

_____

_____

_____

_____

Business Word Bank		
accounting scandal	ethical dilemma	insider trading
assets	ethics	Kyoto Protocol
code of ethics	fair-trade	liabilities
"cooking the books"	fraud	morals
corporate social responsibility	gender discrimination	pay equity
duty to accommodate	glass ceiling	telemarketing fraud
duty to report	grassroots movements	values
embezzlement	harassment	whistle-blower

Use the terms given in the word bank to complete the following statements:

1. The system of personal beliefs and social standards about right and wrong is called

   _____.

2. Our _____ tell us what we think is important, while _____ are the rules we use to decide what's good and what's bad.

3. Businesses develop a(n) _____ to guide employees in a variety of situations.

4. A(n) _____ is a moral problem with a choice between potential right and wrong answers.

5. An employee who informs the public about an ethical violation is a(n) _____.

6. A person or business that lies to the public is guilty of _____.

7. A company perpetrating _____ may use high-pressure phone calls to get customers to donate to a non-existent charity.

8. An audit of U.S. company Enron revealed that it was involved in a(n) _____.

9. _____ is the type of accounting fraud where accountants or senior executives divert company funds for their own gain.

10. An accountant who fraudulently records assets and liabilities is _____.

11. A company's _____ are items that it owns, such as buildings, land, and equipment. On the other hand, a company's _____ are the debts that it owes.

12. A person using confidential information about a company to buy and sell shares is involved in _____.

13. Businesses can exhibit _____ through their values, their ethics, and the contributions they make to their communities.

14. Because corporations have a(n) _____, they must disclose any significant information to shareholders, business partners, lenders, insurers, communities, regulators, consumers, employees, and investors.

15. Women are more likely than men to face _____ in the workplace.

16. Women, minorities, and disabled workers may face a(n) _____ in their desire to reach senior leadership positions.

17. Bullying, stalking, verbal insults, and ridicule are examples of _____.

18. An employer's obligation to eliminate discrimination against employees is known as the _____.

19. The _____ is the agreement reached by countries worldwide to reduce greenhouses gases in the atmosphere.

20. _____ legislation requires employers to provide equal pay for work of equal value.

21. Buying _____ coffee helps producers in developing countries receive a fair profit.

22. _____ develop from the bottom and spread up.

CHAPTER 4: INTERNATIONAL BUSINESS

A. Business Vocabulary

In Chapter 4, you'll encounter some terms related to international business. Before you begin working with the chapter, browse through the pages and look for the bolded key terms. Use the left-hand side of the chart below to write any words you don't immediately understand. Then, when you arrive at the section featuring the word, write its definition in the middle column. Use the last column to note any relevant examples.

Term	Textbook Definition	Examples

B. Chapter Notes: What Is International Business?

Read the first section, What Is International Business? (pages 113–127), in your textbook, and use the following organizers to help guide your note-taking. Then answer the questions that follow.

1. Explain why a business would want to enter the international market.

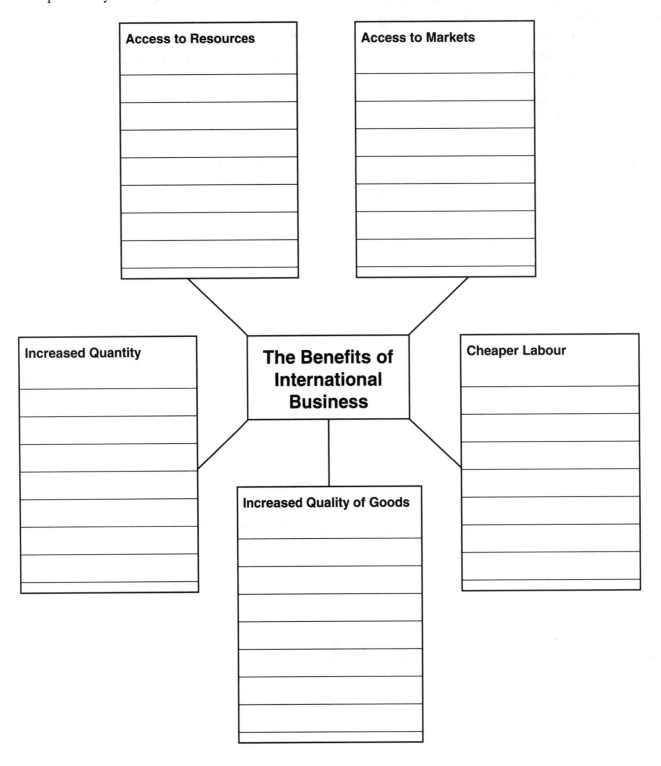

2. The five Ps of international business represent the benefits of getting involved with businesses outside of Canada. Use the graphic organizer below to explain each of the five Ps.

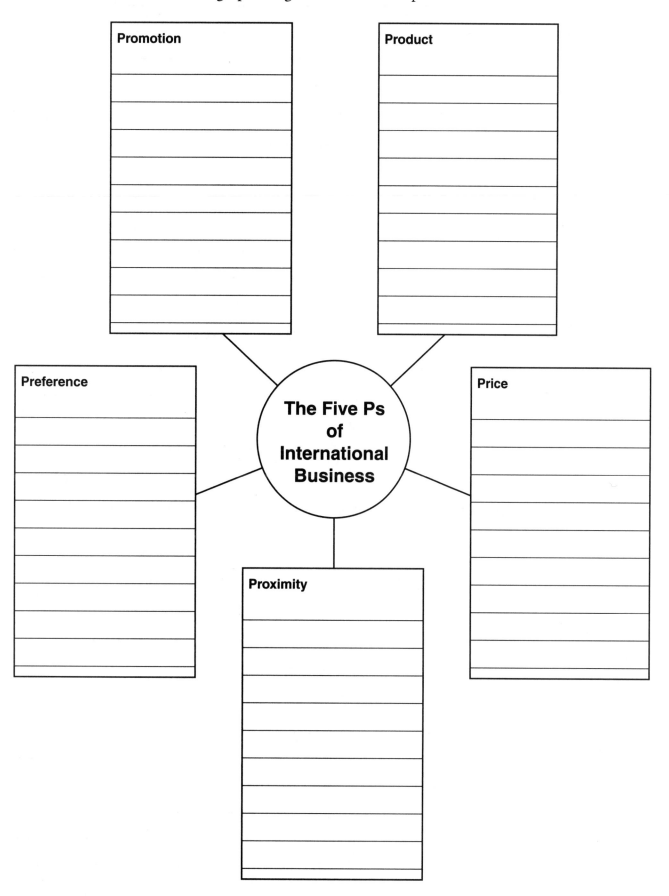

3. Explain what is meant by "social costs" of doing business internationally.

_____

_____

_____

_____

_____

4. Why would a business consider offshore outsourcing? What types of jobs are typically outsourced?

_____

_____

_____

_____

_____

5. List two examples of ethical problems that can result from offshore outsourcing.

_____

_____

_____

_____

_____

6. Explain sustainable development. Why is it important for a business to practise sustainable development?

_____

_____

_____

_____

_____

7. What barriers exist to international business? Why do they exist?

_____

_____

_____

_____

_____

8. What is a tariff? Explain the role of tariffs in managing trade with other countries.

_____

_____

_____

_____

_____

9. Explain the difference between tariff barriers and non-tariff barriers. Name two ways that a country can impose non-tariff barriers.

_____

_____

_____

_____

_____

10. Explain landed cost.

_____

_____

_____

_____

_____

11. List three reasons why governments impose excise taxes.

_____

_____

_____

_____

_____

12. What effect do currency exchange rates have on doing business internationally?

_____

_____

_____

_____

_____

C. Activity: How International Business Affects Everyday Life

To examine the ways in which you and your community rely on and are affected by international business, imagine that you are restricted to purchasing Canadian-made goods and services. With a partner or in a small group, discuss how this restriction would affect each of the following:

a) Your diet:

_____

_____

_____

_____

_____

_____

b) Your entertainment:

_____

_____

_____

_____

_____

_____

c) Your family's transportation:

_____

_____

_____

_____

_____

_____

d) Your overall quality of life:

_____

_____

_____

_____

_____

_____

D. Activity: Exchange Rates

Exchange rates can be used to compare the value of one country's currency to the value of another. For example, on April 10, 2007, one Canadian dollar was equivalent to $0.869 USD. You would need $1.74 USD to buy $2.00 CAD (multiply $2.00 CAD by $0.869 = $1.74 USD).

1. Use the Internet or the financial pages of a major newspaper to find today's exchange rates. For each country listed below, find out the name of its currency, its three-letter currency designation, and how much of this currency you could buy with $500.00 CAD.

Country	Name of Currency	Three-Letter Currency Designation	Exchange Rate	Amount of Currency Equal to $500 Canadian
United States				
Mexico				
Japan				
Taiwan				
Brazil				
Argentina				
United Kingdom				
France				
Turkey				
Thailand				
Jamaica				
Slovakia				

2. Which country's currency is worth the least compared to the Canadian dollar? Identify the country and the currency.

_____

_____

_____

3. Which country's currency is worth the most compared to the Canadian dollar? Identify the country and the currency.

_____

_____

_____

E. Chapter Notes: Flow of Goods and Services

Read the second section, Flow of Goods and Services (pages 128–133), in your textbook, and answer the following questions.

1. Make a list of the goods that come into Canada.

   _____

   _____

2. Explain why governments prefer to have trade surpluses instead of trade deficits.

   _____

   _____

   _____

   _____

   _____

3. Explain the difference between direct and indirect exporting. What type of company is likely to use each type of exporting?

   _____

   _____

   _____

   _____

   _____

   _____

4. Explain five ways a business can offset the risks of importing.

   _____

   _____

   _____

   _____

   _____

   _____

5. What agencies can help exporters learn more about foreign markets?

   _____

   _____

   _____

6. List three reasons why the United States is Canada's number one trading partner.

   _____

   _____

   _____

   _____

F. Activity: Imports and Exports

1. The table below summarizes Canada's imports and exports for the period from 2001 to 2006. Complete the table by determining whether Canada has a trade surplus or a trade deficit in each year. Note that figures in the table are expressed in millions of dollars. For example, the total imports for 2006 were $404 535.0 million, or $404 535 000 000 (just over $400 billion).

Canada's Imports and Exports of Goods
(in millions of dollars)

	2001	2002	2003	2004	2005	2006
Exports	420 730.4	414 038.5	398 953.8	429 120.9	453 060.1	458 166.9
United States[1]	352 165.0	347 051.8	329 000.3	350 751.0	368 577.3	361 308.7
Japan	10 120.8	10 115.0	9 800.7	9 950.6	10 470.5	10 760.8
United Kingdom	6 910.3	6 161.5	7 695.8	9 425.8	9 683.2	11 838.5
European Union	16 688.9	16 294.3	16 414.5	17 351.9	19 206.8	21 719.0
Other OECD[2]	12 172.5	12 670.7	12 751.1	14 399.1	15 245.5	18 379.2
Other Countries[3]	22 672.9	21 745.2	23 291.5	27 243.1	29 876.9	34 160.6
Imports	350 071.2	356 727.1	342 691.9	363 638.5	388 210.3	404 535.0
United States[1]	254 330.7	255 232.5	240 340.4	250 515.6	259 783.9	264 777.6
Japan	10 571.9	11 732.6	10 645.1	10 096.9	11 214.3	11 877.1
United Kingdom	11 954.1	10 181.3	9 180.9	9 466.3	9 061.6	9 685.1
European Union	23 197.1	25 867.0	25 999.6	27 012.3	29 285.6	32 489.4
Other OECD[2]	18 649.8	19 686.6	19 695.3	22 254.1	24 308.8	23 724.5
Other Countries[3]	31 367.2	34 027.1	36 830.7	44 293.2	54 556.1	61 981.4
Trade Deficit/ Surplus						
United States[1]						
Japan						
United Kingdom						
European Union						
Other OECD[2]						
Other Countries[3]						

1. Includes Puerto Rico and Virgin Islands.

2. Organization for Economic Co-operation and Development, excluding the United States, Japan, United Kingdom, and other European Union countries.

3. Countries not included in the European Union or the Organization for Economic Co-operation and Development (OECD).

Source: Statistics Canada

2. Describe Canada's trading relationship with each of the following countries, for the period 2001–2006. Use the words *trade deficit* or *trade surplus* in your answers.

a) United States:

_____

_____

_____

_____

_____

b) Japan:

_____

_____

_____

_____

_____

c) United Kingdom:

_____

_____

_____

_____

_____

d) European Union:

_____

_____

_____

_____

_____

3. Canada's largest trading partner is the United States. Explain how this relationship influences the balance of trade in Canada.

_____

_____

_____

_____

_____

G. Chapter Notes: Canada and International Trade Agreements

Read the third section, Canada and International Trade Agreements (pages 134–139), in your textbook, and answer the following questions.

1. List two advantages of reducing trade barriers between countries.

_____

_____

_____

_____

_____

_____

_____

2. What characteristics of trade are outlined in a trade agreement?

_____

_____

_____

_____

_____

_____

3. What is GATT? What was its original intent?

_____

_____

_____

_____

_____

_____

4. What is the role of the World Trade Organization (WTO)? Why was it established?

_____

_____

_____

_____

_____

5. Outline the goals of the Canada–U.S. Free Trade Agreement (FTA) for each country.

   a) Canada:

   _____

   _____

   _____

   _____

   _____

   b) United States:

   _____

   _____

   _____

   _____

   _____

6. List three benefits and five concerns about NAFTA.

   a) Benefits:
      1. _____

      _____

      2. _____

      _____

      3. _____

      _____

   b) Concerns:
      1. _____

      _____

      2. _____

      _____

      3. _____

      _____

      4. _____

      _____

      5. _____

      _____

7. How is a bilateral agreement different from a regional trade agreement?

_____

_____

_____

_____

_____

8. What is a trading bloc? Provide an example.

_____

_____

_____

_____

_____

9. What countries make up the Group of Eight (G8)? What is the purpose of this association?

_____

_____

_____

_____

_____

_____

_____

_____

10. List four other trade agreements that Canada has an interest in and explain this interest.

_____

_____

_____

_____

_____

_____

_____

_____

_____

H. Activity: Trade Agreements

1. For each product listed, determine the trade agreement that governs, or will govern, its trade between the countries listed.

Product	Trading Countries	Relevant Trade Agreement(s)
T-shirts	Canada and Mexico	
Gold	Canada and Norway	
Shoes	China and United States	
Chocolate	Switzerland and Iceland	
Coffee	Brazil and Mexico	
Books	Canada and United States	
Electronics	Japan and China	
Rum	Jamaica and The Bahamas	
Shrimp	El Salvador and Belize	
Aircraft parts	United States and Mexico	

2. The North American Free Trade Agreement (NAFTA) joined Canada, the United States, and Mexico in a continent-wide free-trade zone. For each scenario below, determine whether duty would apply to each trade.

Company Ownership	Country of Manufacture	Country of Export	Will duty apply?
Canada	Mexico	United States	
Canada	China	Mexico	
Mexico	Mexico	United States	
United States	United States	Canada	
United States	Belgium	Canada	
Japan	China	United States	
Canada	Canada	United States	
France	Taiwan	Mexico	

I. Chapter Notes: The Future of International Trade

Read the fourth section, The Future of International Trade (pages 140–145), in your textbook, and answer the following questions.

1. In what ways are NAFTA and the EU different?

_____

_____

_____

2. The future of international trade depends, in part, on our ability to accept and respond to cultural differences. Use the table below to list the cultural factors that need to be considered when doing business with other countries. Rank each factor according to what you believe is most important. Explain your rationale for each ranking.

Rank	Factor	Explanation
1		
2		
3		
4		
5		

3. What is global dependency? Provide an example.

_____

_____

_____

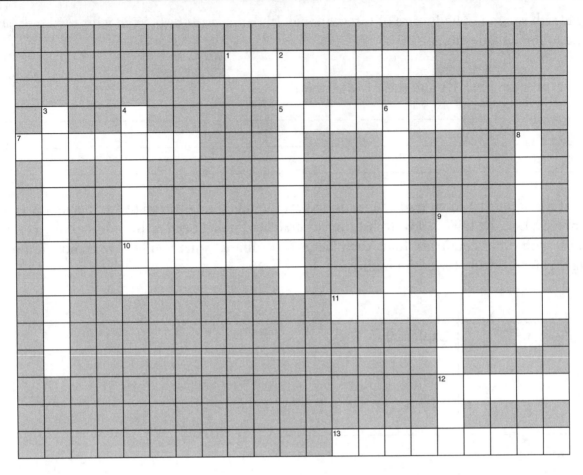

Across

1. _____-making processes vary from country to country.

5. Criteria for good _____ vary from culture to culture.

7. A _____ in one country could mean something very different in another country.

10. When dealing with other cultures, it is important to show _____ for their beliefs and customs.

11. In many cultures, _____ communication signals tell a lot about a situation.

12. The trade agreement between Canada, the United States, and Mexico is called _____.

13. A _____ is a common way to greet someone.

Down

2. International business plays a vital role in our global _____.

3. Customers demanding items that are created in another country are demonstrating global _____.

4. The sum of a country's way of life, beliefs, and customs is called its _____.

6. The EU is a union of many _____ countries into a single market.

8. When you do something at the agreed time, you are _____.

9. First impressions are often formed based on initial _____.

K. Case Study: The Great Bicycle Tariff Debate

In 2005, the Canadian International Trade Tribunal (CITT) recommended adding a 30 percent surtax on imported bicycles after receiving complaints from the Canadian Bicycle Manufacturers Association (CBMA). The CBMA's two members, Groupe Procycle Inc. and Raleigh Canada Ltd., claimed that rising foreign imports of bicycles, particularly from China, were damaging their businesses and they could no longer effectively compete in the Canadian marketplace. They warned that, without help, factories would have to be closed and up to 600 workers would be laid off.

Independent bicycle retailers, however, did not agree with the recommendation. They argued that a surtax on bicycles would drive up prices and drive away customers, and could ultimately cost the jobs of up to 5000 people employed in the retail bicycle industry. It should have come as no surprise that the proposed surtax met with a lot of resistance, as Canada already boasts the highest bicycle tariffs of any country in the world, with two levels of tariff already in place.

As debate over the tariff grew more heated, bicycle-friendly initiatives were being implemented across the country to encourage people to use this greener method of transportation. Critics of the surtax argued that, in a country where gasoline prices, smog, and traffic congestion were on the rise, adding an additional surtax to a clean and affordable solution would be foolish.

The following year, the federal government overturned the recommendation of the CITT, citing increased costs for retailers and consumers, which would harm the economy and would ultimately not provide a long-term solution for the bicycle manufacturers in this case.

1. Explain the potential negative economic impact of imposing a tariff on imported bicycles.

_____

_____

2. What type of barrier was proposed and why?

_____

_____

_____

3. List at least two arguments for and against implementing the tariff.

Arguments for Implementing the Tariff	Arguments against Implementing the Tariff

Business Word Bank		
balance of trade	global economy	social costs
bilateral	global products	sustainable development
culture	Group of Eight (G8)	tariffs
direct exporting	indirect exporting	trade agreements
domestic transaction	International Labour Organization	trade deficit
environmental degradation	international transaction	trade surplus
five Ps	landed cost	trading bloc
foreign trade	NAFTA	transnational
global dependency	non-tariff barrier	World Trade Organization

Use the terms given in the word bank to complete the following statements:

1. A(n) _____ is the selling of items produced in the same country. Selling items produced in others countries is a(n) _____.

2. _____ involves the exchange of goods and services across national borders.

3. When you participate in an international transaction, you are contributing to the _____.

4. Standardized products, such as basketballs, ballpoint pens, and cotton cloth are examples of _____.

5. The _____ of international business are product, price, proximity, preference, and promotion.

6. The _____ of international business include offshore outsourcing, human rights or labour abuses, and environmental degradation.

7. _____ companies, such as Nike and Honda, operate in several countries.

8. The United Nations specialized agency that seeks the promotion of social justice and tries to protect internationally recognized human rights and labour rights is the _____.

9. The process of development that tries not to damage the environment or exhaust natural resources for the future is known as _____.

10. The consumption of natural resources faster than nature can replenish them is known as
_____.

11. Customs duties or _____ are a tax on goods imported into Canada.

12. Setting high standards for imported automobiles is an example of a(n) _____.

13. The _____ is the actual cost for an imported item purchased, composed of the vendor cost, transportation charges, duties, taxes, broker fees, and any other charges.

14. Countries try to maintain a(n) _____ between the value of products they import and the value of products they export.

15. A country that pays more for imports than it earns for exports is facing a(n)
_____, while a country that earns more from exports than it pays for imports has a(n) _____.

16. When shipping goods to another country, an established company is more likely to engage in
_____ and deal directly with an importer. A new company is more likely to use an intermediary, thereby engaging in _____.

17. Countries enter into _____ to make trade easier by reducing trade barriers.

18. The _____ was established in 1995 to govern international trade.

19. _____ is the trade agreement between Canada, the United States, and Mexico that allows freer trade between the three countries.

20. A(n) _____ trade agreement involves two parties or two countries.

21. A(n) _____ is a group of countries that share the same trade interests.

22. The _____, an association of the world's most powerful industrialized democracies, meets annually to discuss major economic and political issues.

23. A country's _____ is composed of its way of life, beliefs, and customs.

24. Consumers' demands for goods created in other countries are a sign of _____.

CHAPTER 5: PRODUCTION

A. Business Vocabulary

In Chapter 5, you'll encounter some terms related to production. Before you begin working with the chapter, browse through the pages and look for the bolded key terms. Use the left-hand side of the chart below to write any words you don't immediately understand. Then, when you arrive at the section featuring the word, write its definition in the middle column. Use the last column to note any relevant examples.

Term	Textbook Definition	Examples

Read the first section, Factors of Production (pages 155–161), in your textbook, and answer the following questions.

1. Everything in the world is made from only six types of natural resources. List these resources.

   _____

   _____

2. Briefly describe each of the six factors of production.

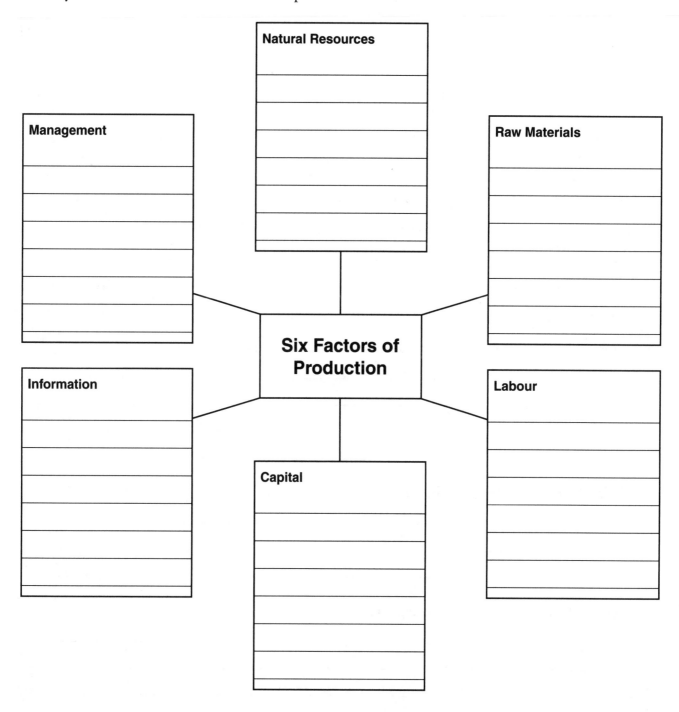

3. Use the Venn diagram to explain the difference between ingredients and supplies. Provide an example of each.

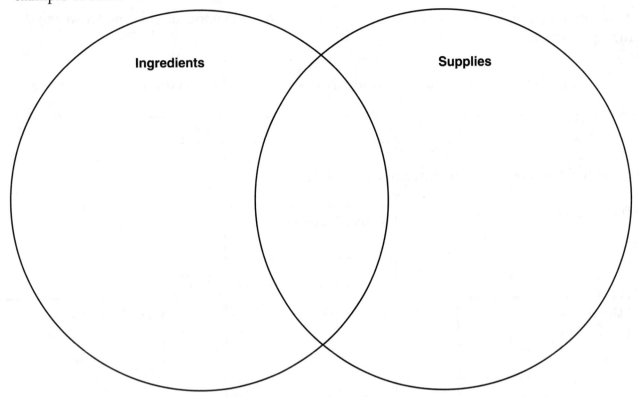

Ingredients   **Supplies**

4. To save on labour costs, a business can

   a) _____

   b) _____

   c) _____

5. Explain the two types of capital, and provide two examples of each.

   _____

   _____

   _____

   _____

6. Explain how information can be a commodity.

   _____

   _____

   _____

7. What tasks are performed by management?

   _____

   _____

   _____

C. Activity: What Am I?

Use the clues to help you figure out the identity of a factor of production and provide an example of each one.

information	liquid capital	processing
ingredients	management	raw materials
intellectual property	natural resources	supplies
labour		

1. You'll find me on the packaging of most foods. _____

   Example: _____

2. It is easy to spend my resources. _____

   Example: _____

3. I make the decisions about how to use my company's resources. _____

   Example: _____

4. You can save on my costs by automating tasks. _____

   Example: _____

5. Everything in the world is made from me. _____

   Example: _____

6. You need me to keep your business clean. _____

   Example: _____

7. You can charge companies to advertise on a website featuring me. _____

   Example: _____

8. Although you can't see me, I am part of a business's non-liquid capital. _____

   Example: _____

9. I take natural resources and convert them into other products. _____

   Example: _____

10. You can use me to make other goods. _____

    Example: _____

D. Chapter Notes: The Production Process

Read the second section, The Production Process (pages 162–166), in your textbook, and answer the following questions.

1. List the four stages of the production process.

   _____

   _____

   _____

   _____

2. What factors do you need to consider when determining what raw materials to purchase?

   _____

   _____

   _____

3. Explain what refining does and when it may be used.

   _____

   _____

   _____

4. Why might certain products have to meet government standards of quality?

   _____

   _____

   _____

   _____

5. Explain the purpose of the International Organization for Standardization (ISO).

   _____

   _____

   _____

   _____

   _____

6. How does grading help consumers make informed judgments about a purchase?

   _____

   _____

   _____

E. Activity: You Are the Purchaser

Imagine that you have been hired to do the purchasing for a fast-food restaurant chain. For each item below, consider the quality, costs, and hidden costs. Select the company you will buy from, and explain why you made that selection.

a) **Hamburgers—500 000 needed**

Company	Quality	Price/Unit	Hidden Costs/Unit	Total Cost/ Unit	Total Cost
Company A	Average	50¢	1¢		
Company B	Average	40¢	8¢		
Company C	Good	60¢	3¢		

Which company will you buy from? Justify your choice.

_____

_____

b) **Cups—1 million needed**

Company	Quality	Price/Unit	Hidden Costs/Unit	Total Cost/ Unit	Total Cost
Company D	Good	5¢	1.5¢		
Company E	Average	3¢	1.0¢		
Company F	Poor	1¢	0.5¢		

Which company will you buy from? Justify your choice.

_____

_____

c) **Takeout containers—20 000 needed**

Company	Quality	Price/Unit	Hidden Costs/Unit	Total Cost/ Unit	Total Cost
Company G	Good	22¢	1¢		
Company H	Poor	20¢	3¢		
Company I	Poor	21¢	2¢		

Which company will you buy from? Justify your choice.

_____

_____

F. Chapter Notes: Improving Productivity

Read the third section, Improving Productivity (pages 166–171), in your textbook, and use the following organizer to help guide your note-taking. Then answer the questions that follow.

1. Define each of the following factors and explain how it can increase productivity.

Factor	How can it improve productivity?
Training	
Capital Investment	
Investment in Technology	
New Inventory Systems	

2. List three ways that quality and speed can influence productivity.

_____

_____

_____

3. How can increased productivity actually decrease profitability?

_____

_____

_____

G. Activity: Increasing Productivity

For each situation below, explain one way to increase productivity within the business.

1. A bakery's management finds that the bakery produces half as many baked goods as its competitors.

   _____

   _____

   _____

   _____

   _____

2. Employees feel frustrated because new systems are constantly implemented, and they do not feel confident in applying them.

   _____

   _____

   _____

   _____

3. A company finds that it has either too many or too few of the raw materials required for production.

   _____

   _____

   _____

   _____

4. A grocery store's management finds that the store's shelves are often empty because they never know how much inventory they have.

   _____

   _____

   _____

   _____

5. A salesperson is on the road often but needs access to e-mail regularly.

   _____

   _____

   _____

   _____

Take a look at these two Japanese characters. Can you spot the difference? Both are pronounced Jidoka. Taiichi Ohno, one of the engineers who founded Toyota in Japan, considered Jidoka one of the two pillars of the Toyota Production System (TPS). The original meaning of Jidoka was automation: the use of automatic controls to operate machines. It was written in Kanji script as shown on the left. Toyota's Kamigo Engine Plant developed many stoppage devices to halt automated machines when problems arise, coining the term "autonomation" for this process. Though autonomation was also known as Jidoka, the way it was written in Kanji had a subtle difference—the addition of a few strokes representing humans or people.

Autonomation means automation with human intelligence, where devices on a production line have the ability to shut down a process when a part is defective or a mechanism jams. This allows equipment to run without constant human attention, allowing workers to staff multiple operations.

Jidoka, when applied to manual assembly, refers to the practice of stopping an entire production line or process when something goes amiss. Traditionally, workers had no responsibility for what came off the line. As long as a worker completed the task assigned by the overseer, there was no expectation that the worker take any interest in what else was going on. Workers were to be like machines— silent, repetitive, always working. But under Jidoka, in essence, everyone is now an overseer. It is the human element in the production process. Machines don't think but people do. It's not that workers *can* stop the line—workers *must* stop the line. Everyone is responsible in the production process.

What would it take to make you stop a production line? If you stopped the line, everyone would have to stop what they were doing and you would have to immediately identify what was wrong. Would you take that step? It requires a courage of conviction that many people do not possess. Wouldn't it be easier to just keep doing your job and let it go? Someone else—a manager, supervisor, or quality control officer—could find the problem. As long as you do your job correctly, does it matter? This is the heart of Jidoka. It is the key idea in the pursuit of "continuous improvement."

1. How are the three definitions of Jidoka different? How are they similar?

_____

_____

_____

_____

_____

_____

_____

_____

2. Why would it be a problem for one person to stop an entire production line? Think about some reasons why people would not stop the line. Share your reasons with a peer. Are they similar?

_____

_____

_____

_____

_____

_____

_____

_____

3. Explain how Jidoka can help ensure that a product conforms to specific standards.

_____

_____

_____

_____

_____

_____

_____

_____

I. Review

Business Word Bank		
automated	intellectual property	processing
capital	just-in-time	quality control
consolidated	labour	raw materials
extractive industries	liquid	refining
grading	management	supplies
ingredients		

Use the terms given in the word bank to complete the following statements:

1. Industries that take something out of the earth or sea are called _____.

2. _____ are goods that are used to produce other goods.

3. The making of a Ganong chocolate uses _____ such as sugar and cocoa. _____ are used to maintain the machines that make the chocolates.

4. Wheat milled into flour is an example of _____.

5. _____ is the physical and mental effort needed to produce goods or services.

6. To save on labour costs, many tasks once performed by people are now _____.

7. Tim Hortons _____ its bakery operations when it opened a large plant to bake all of its products.

8. _____ is the money invested in a business. If it is _____, it can easily be turned into something else.

9. A business's trade secrets or the ideas or talent of its work force is its _____.

10. _____ controls the factors of production and allots a company's resources.

11. _____ is a process that turns oil into gasoline.

12. _____ departments ensure products meet certain standards for use.

13. Gasoline and eggs are examples of goods that are subject to _____.

14. A(n) _____ inventory system allows a business to have the goods it needs, where it needs them, when it needs them.

CHAPTER 6: HUMAN RESOURCES

A. Business Vocabulary

In Chapter 6, you'll encounter some terms related to human resources. Before you begin working with the chapter, browse through the pages and look for the bolded key terms. Use the left-hand side of the chart below to write any words you don't immediately understand. Then, when you arrive at the section featuring the word, write its definition in the middle column. Use the last column to note any relevant examples.

Term	Textbook Definition	Examples

B. Chapter Notes: The Functions of Human Resources Management

Read the first section, The Functions of Human Resources Management (pages 178–194), in your textbook, and answer the following questions.

1. What is the role of a human resources department?

   _____

   _____

   _____

   _____

   _____

   _____

2. Explain why employers are considered buyers of skills and employees sellers of skills in the labour market.

   _____

   _____

   _____

   _____

   _____

   _____

3. Explain the four types of labour, and provide an example of each.

   1. _____

      _____

   2. _____

      _____

   3. _____

      _____

   4. _____

      _____

4. Why would a business want workers to be more productive?

   _____

   _____

   _____

5. Explain why businesses prefer to hire skilled employees.

_____

_____

_____

_____

_____

6. What factors do human resources managers consider when predicting a company's personnel needs?

_____

_____

_____

_____

_____

7. In what situations will human resources managers look outside the company to fill positions? What methods can they use to find employees?

_____

_____

_____

_____

_____

_____

8. What does an interview team try to learn about an applicant during an interview?

_____

_____

_____

_____

9. What are new employees typically taught during their orientation at a new company?

_____

_____

_____

_____

_____

10. Why would employee turnover be a problem for a business? How could an employer go about keeping good employees?

_____

_____

_____

_____

11. Discuss the three ways in which employees may leave a business for which they work.

1. _____

_____

2. _____

_____

3. _____

_____

12. Discuss the actions that may be taken when an employee is not fulfilling duties as required.

_____

_____

_____

_____

_____

13. Explain the various forms that compensation can take.

a) Hourly wages

_____

_____

b) Salary

_____

_____

c) Salary plus commission

_____

_____

d) Straight commission

_____

_____

e) Incentive bonus

_____

_____

f) Performance-based pay

_____

_____

g) Fee for service

_____

_____

h) Royalty or licensing fee

_____

_____

i) Stock options

_____

_____

14. List four reasons why it is beneficial for a business to provide a healthy and safe work environment.

1. _____

_____

2. _____

_____

3. _____

_____

4. _____

_____

15. What safety precautions should be taken in the workplace?

_____

_____

_____

_____

_____

_____

_____

C. Activity: My Job

Answer the following questions about a job you have been paid to do. If you have never had a paying job, consider your household chores or any volunteer work you have participated in.

1. Describe the job. What were your duties?

   _____

   _____

2. How did you get the job?

   _____

   _____

3. How were you paid? How often?

   _____

   _____

4. Were there any benefits involved in working at this job (e.g., discounts, health care, free meals)?

   _____

   _____

5. What kinds of skills were required for this job? How did you acquire them?

   _____

   _____

   _____

6. Were there any health and safety risks involved in this job? If so, what were these risks and how did you protect yourself from harm?

   _____

   _____

   _____

7. If you no longer work at this job, under what circumstances did you leave?

   _____

   _____

8. What experiences will you take from this job to use in another job?

   _____

   _____

D. Activity: How Much Will You Get Paid?

For each scenario below, determine how much you would get paid.

1. As a retail employee, you are earning $8.50 per hour. You have worked 22 hours in the past two weeks. What would your paycheque be if no deductions were taken? If 10 percent of your cheque was deducted for taxes, what would be the amount of your paycheque?

    _____

    _____

    _____

2. You've just landed a full-time office job that pays you $500.00 per week before taxes. What is your annual income before taxes?

    _____

    _____

    _____

3. As a salesperson, you earn $9.00 per hour plus 1 percent commission. This month you've worked 57 hours and have sold $8000.00 in goods. How much would you earn before taxes?

    _____

    _____

    _____

4. You work as a telephone interviewer and get paid $2.10 for every survey you complete. The first night you complete 19 surveys. The rest of the week is slow and you only complete an additional 14 surveys. How much will you earn this week before taxes?

    _____

    _____

    _____

5. A client asks your catering company to provide a quote on a three-course dinner for 100 people. You know that it will cost you $26.00 per person in raw materials, and estimate that it will take 12 hours for your eight-person staff to cook the food. Each member of your staff earns $10.00 per hour. How much should you quote if you want to make a 15 percent profit?

    _____

    _____

    _____

    _____

Read the second section, Key Employability Skills (pages 194–197), in your textbook, and use the following organizer to help guide your note-taking.

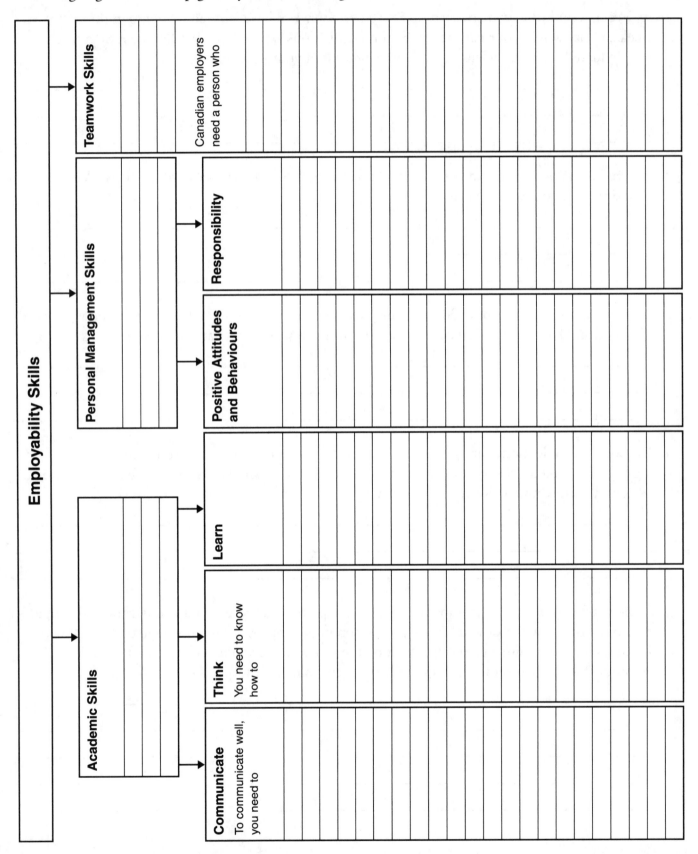

Employability Skills

Teamwork Skills

Canadian employers need a person who

Personal Management Skills

Responsibility

Positive Attitudes and Behaviours

Academic Skills

Learn

Think
You need to know how to

Communicate
To communicate well, you need to

F. Activity: My Employability Skills

For each of the employability skills below, determine whether you have the skill, what you can do to improve the skill, and what you can do to develop the skill if you don't currently posses it.

Skill	Do I have this skill?	How can I improve this skill?	What can I do to develop this skill?
Academic Skills			
• read, comprehend, and use written materials, including graphs, charts, and displays			
• write effectively in the languages in which business is conducted			
• think critically and act logically to evaluate situations, solve problems, and make decisions			
Personal Management Skills			
• a positive attitude toward learning, growth, and personal health			
• the ability to plan and manage time, money, and other resources to achieve goals			
• a positive attitude toward change			
Teamwork Skills			
• exercise "give and take" to achieve group goals			
• respect the thoughts and opinions of others in the group			
• lead where appropriate, mobilizing the group for high performance			

G. Chapter Notes: Business Careers

Read the third section, Business Careers (pages 197–200), in your textbook, and use the following organizer to help guide your note-taking.

In the business world, there are a variety of careers to choose from. In the organizer below, briefly describe each type of career and provide two examples of jobs that are associated with the field.

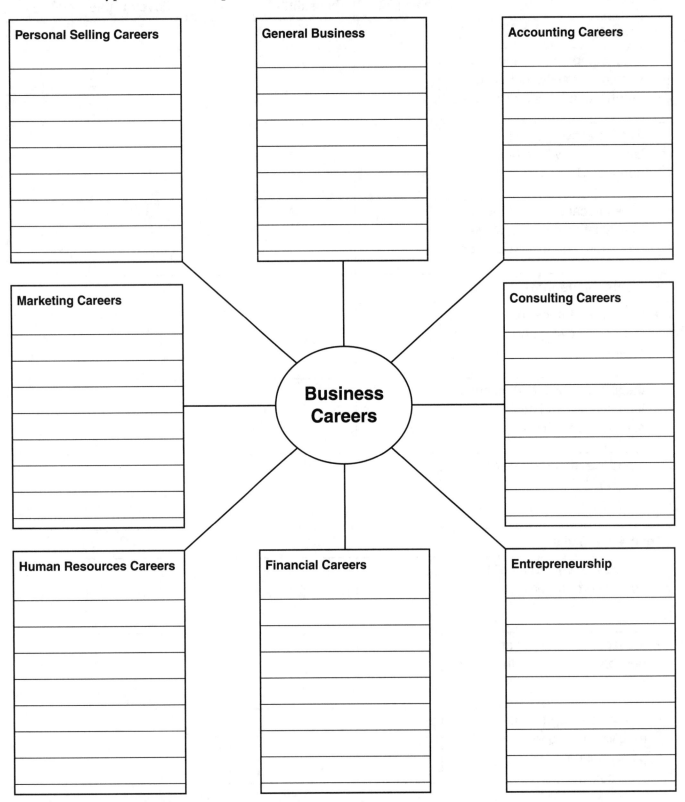

Personal Selling Careers

General Business

Accounting Careers

Marketing Careers

Business Careers

Consulting Careers

Human Resources Careers

Financial Careers

Entrepreneurship

H. Activity: What Skills Are Required?

1. For each profession below, think about the skills that are best suited to the job. Place an x in the box for each skill you believe is required for the career.

Profession	Multitasking	Creativity	Math Skills	People Skills	Teamwork Skills	Research Skills	Sales Skills
Loan officer							
Waiter							
Human resources manager							
Event planner							
Real estate agent							
Cashier							
Entrepreneur							
Business consultant							
Advertising executive							
Landscaper							
Travel agent							

2. For which jobs do you think you possess most of the required skills? Are there any jobs you hadn't considered before?

_____

_____

_____

_____

_____

_____

I. Chapter Notes: Rights in the Workplace

Read the fourth section, Rights in the Workplace (pages 201–204), in your textbook, and answer the following question.

The provincial and federal governments have drafted legislation that sets out employment standards for workers in the private and public sectors. What are the rights of an employee as expressed in the Universal Declaration of Human Rights and the *Ontario Human Rights Code*?

_____

_____

_____

_____

_____

_____

_____

_____

_____

_____

_____

_____

_____

_____

_____

_____

_____

_____

_____

_____

_____

_____

_____

_____

_____

_____

J. Activity: Can You Do This in the Workplace?

For each situation below, explain whether the action is lawful or unlawful based on employee and employer rights, and explain why.

Situation	Lawful	Unlawful	Explanation
An employer dismisses an employee because he is negligent.			
An employee is dismissed because she is pregnant.			
A male employee is paid less than a female employee for the same work.			
A group of employees wishes to start a union.			
An employee is teased because of his sexual orientation.			
An employer offers to pay a new employee below minimum wage for a retail job.			
Although she is the most qualified applicant, a person is not hired by an employer because she is in a wheelchair.			
An employee seeks time off to be with his new baby.			
An employer refuses to hire a 12-year-old to work for her.			

Bradner Village is a health care centre and retirement community in Northeast Indiana that has 230 full-time employees who serve more than 200 residents. Despite spending thousands of dollars on training and development for new hires, Bradner Village executives saw high employee turnover and frustration among employees. In recent years, Bradner lost almost half of its full-time staff. Staffing executives had difficulty finding qualified candidates to fill positions.

In 2004, Bradner president and CEO Eric Walts and human resources manager Deborah Raver decided to address this ongoing crisis. With guidance from the Northeast Indiana Workforce Investment Board (NIWIB), Bradner used the WorkKeys system to profile four key positions—licensed nurses, certified nursing assistants, dietary staff, and environmental services staff. It also identified the minimum WorkKeys-related skill level scores required for entry into each job.

Prior to job interviews, applicants went to the NIWIB's local WorkOne office, where they took WorkKeys exams in Applied Mathematics, Locating Information, Observation, and Reading for Information. Candidates who met the profile standards qualified for a job interview.

Results

- *Greater supervisory satisfaction and reduction in turnover*—Bradner's key issue was high turnover rates. In a six-month period in 2004, Bradner lost 73 employees. In the same six-month period in 2005, after WorkKeys implementation, it lost only 46. This is a 37 percent reduction in turnover.

- *Tremendous training costs savings*—All new certified nursing assistants at Bradner Village are required to complete three weeks of on-site training. Before WorkKeys, this training was offered every month to a class of 20 new hires. Fewer than 50 percent of those hires would make it through the course and work at Bradner Village, creating a loss of more than $86 000 per year. WorkKeys helped Bradner identify candidates likely to succeed in the certified nursing assistants training. Most employees hired now complete the training and stay with the company. Retention is high enough that Bradner has been able to reduce its training to once every two months for smaller classes of about 15. This reduced Bradner's training losses to a mere $3600 a year—a 96 percent training-cost reduction.

- *Time savings in the selection process*—Before WorkKeys, Bradner's human resources department typically spent much of its workweek wading through applications. Identifying qualified applicants was like "shooting a dartboard with a blindfold on," human resources manager Raver said. Now Raver selects only applicants who meet the WorkKeys job requirements. To identify 25 qualified applicants now takes only two hours, instead of eight—a time saving of 75 percent. She also is able to offer jobs to 95 percent of candidates she interviews—a 55 percent improvement in identifying qualified applicants.

1. What category of labour was Bradner Village seeking? How do you know?

_____

_____

_____

_____

_____

_____

_____

2. What were the benefits to the company in implementing WorkKeys?

_____

_____

_____

_____

_____

_____

_____

3. Why might employee turnover have decreased with the implementation of WorkKeys?

_____

_____

_____

_____

_____

_____

_____

4. What else could the company do to retain good employees?

_____

_____

_____

_____

_____

_____

_____

L. Review

Business Word Bank		
bonus	incentive	royalty
commission	labour market	salary
compensation	minimum wage	sales quota
corrective interview	occupational forecast	semiskilled labour
employee layoffs	orientation	seniority
employee referral program	overtime	severance package
employee turnover	perks	sick pay
exit interview	pension	skilled labour
harassment	piecework	sweatshops
headhunter	professional labour	unskilled labour
human resources department	protected grounds	wellness programs

Use the terms in the word bank to complete the following statements:

1. The _____ coordinates all activities relating to the company's employees.

2. Employers, buyers of skills, and employees, sellers of skills, meet in the _____.

3. Making predictions about what kinds of jobs will be popular in the future is part of a(n) _____.

4. Jobs that require little training are considered to be _____ while those requiring some training are _____.

5. _____ requires a person who has obtained training through schooling or previous employment; _____ requires people highly trained in specific occupations.

6. _____ is the rate at which employees voluntarily leave a company.

7. A company looking to hire new employees can employ the services of a(n) _____ or institute a(n) _____ to encourage employees to find qualified applicants.

8. During _____ a new employee is introduced to the business's policies.

9. To attract experienced employees, some companies offer _____ such as casual dress codes and daycare services.

10. Sometimes, a(n) _____ is held with a departing employee.

11. A(n) _____ allows an employer and employee to come up with a plan to address job difficulties.

12. A business that needs to reduce its expenses may reduce its workforce through _____.

13. The length of service a person has with a company is known as _____.

14. Many companies provide a dismissed employee with a final payment as part of a _____.

15. A retired employee receives income through his or her _____.

16. _____ is the amount of money and other benefits received by an employee in exchange for work.

17. _____ is the lowest hourly wage an employer can legally pay a worker.

18. Work done beyond a prescribed number of hours is considered _____.

19. Employees paid a fixed amount earn a(n) _____, while employees working on _____ earn a percentage of their sales and have an added _____ to sell more goods.

20. An employee who meets his or her _____ may receive a(n) _____ as a reward.

21. Employees whose wages are based on the amount of work they complete are engaged in _____. In some countries, the factories where these employees work are called _____ because they offer low wages and unsafe working conditions.

22. A songwriter receives a(n) _____ each time his or her song is played.

23. Compensation paid to employees who are away ill is called _____. To reduce the number of employees who are ill, many companies have instituted _____.

24. The characteristics of an employee that, by law, cannot lead to harassment or discrimination are called _____.

25. Rude comments and inappropriate suggestions are examples of _____.

CHAPTER 7: MANAGEMENT

A. Business Vocabulary

In Chapter 7, you'll encounter some terms related to management. Before you begin working with the chapter, browse through the pages and look for the bolded key terms. Use the left-hand side of the chart below to write any words you don't immediately understand. Then, when you arrive at the section featuring the word, write its definition in the middle column. Use the last column to note any relevant examples.

Term	Textbook Definition	Examples

B. Chapter Notes: How Management Functions

Read the first section, How Management Functions (pages 210–214), in your textbook, and use the following organizer to help guide your note-taking.

Management performs four major functions for any business: planning, organizing, leading, and controlling. Define the four functions of management and provide examples of types of activities performed within each area.

Planning	Leading

Organizing	Controlling

C. Activity: You Are the Project Manager

Imagine that you are a contestant on a reality TV show. You have been appointed project manager for your six-person team on the following tasks:

1. Create a new flavour of ice cream sundae for a chain of ice cream shops.

2. Choose a creative name for your sundae.

3. Create an ingredients list.

4. Determine what price you will set for your sundae.

5. Market the product and come up with a strategy to encourage customers to buy it. (Who do you want to market the new flavour to? Where will you sell it? When will you sell the product? How will you go about selling the product?)

6. For each function of management, explain what you, as the project manager, will need to do to win. To be successful, your team must generate more revenue from the sale of your sundae than the other team.

Explain how you would approach each of the four business functions for this project.

Ice cream sundae name: _____

Ingredients: _____

_____

_____

_____

Price: _____

Planning:

_____

_____

_____

_____

_____

_____

_____

_____

_____

_____

_____

Organizing:

_____

_____

_____

_____

_____

_____

Leading:

_____

_____

_____

_____

_____

_____

_____

Controlling:

_____

_____

_____

_____

_____

_____

_____

_____

D. Chapter Notes: Managing Resources

Read the second section, Managing Resources (pages 214–215), in your textbook, and use the following organizer to help guide your note-taking.

Many businesses have a different manager for each resource area. Use the graphic organizer to explain the role of each manager.

Type of Manager	Role of Manager
Purchasing manager	
Production manager	
Marketing and distribution manager	
Research and development manager	
Finance manager	

E. Activity: Expanding the Market

Imagine that you have been hired by a company that sells cookies. Its chocolate chip cookies are selling well, but it would like to expand further into the cookie market and develop some new cookie types. As a member of the research and development department, how would you help the company plan for this expansion? How would the purchasing, production, and marketing and distribution managers play a role in this initiative?

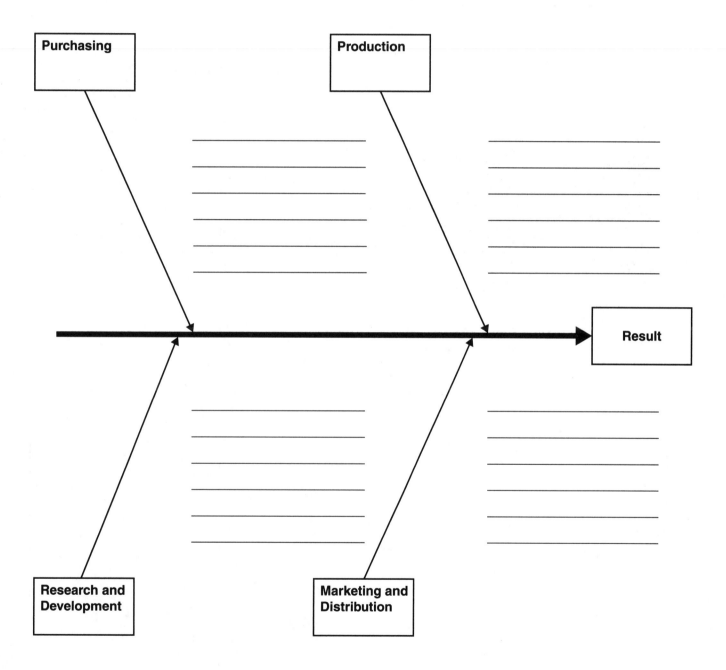

F. Chapter Notes: Leadership Styles

Read the third section, Leadership Styles (pages 216–217), in your textbook, and use the following organizer to help guide your note-taking.

All leaders have different styles depending on their personality and the situation. Define each leadership style, explain when it is most useful, and consider its drawbacks.

Leadership Style	Definition	When it Is Most Useful	Drawbacks
Autocratic leadership			
Laissez-faire leadership			
Democratic leadership			

G. Activity: Should Managers Use Only One Style?

Imagine that you are a manager. Below are some situations that you might face as a manager, and some options you might consider. Circle the option that you feel will best handle the situation. Explain your selection.

Scenario A

The workers in your department are having problems completing their tasks on time. Performance levels have been going steadily downhill for some time. You have tried to be friendly and supportive but with little response from your staff.

What would you do?

1. Discuss the issues with your staff and then set revised performance goals.

2. Emphasize the need for following regular procedures and meeting task expectations and deadlines.

3. Remind staff members that you are available to discuss any problems, but don't put pressure them.

4. Wait and see what happens.

Explanation:

_____

_____

_____

Scenario B

During the past few weeks, the quality of work completed by staff members has been improving. You have been careful to make sure that they are aware of your performance expectations but are considering raising their performance goals.

What would you do?

1. Stay out of the way.

2. Increase staff members' performance goals without consulting them.

3. Be supportive and provide clear feedback.

4. Discuss increasing performance goals with staff members to make them feel important and involved in the decision-making process.

Explanation:

_____

_____

_____

Scenario C

Both performance levels and interpersonal relations in your department have been good. Your usual practice has been to leave your staff alone to do their jobs. Now an issue has come up, and staff members are unable to solve the problem themselves.

What would you do?

1. Arrange to get the group together and work as a team to solve the problem.

2. Continue to leave them alone.

3. Act decisively to identify the problem and provide a solution to correct it.

4. Support your workers while they work on the problem. Let them know you are available as a resource if they need you.

Explanation:

_____

_____

_____

Scenario D

A major change is about to occur in your organization. Staff in your department have a record of accomplishment and commitment to excellence and are supportive of the need for change.

What would you do?

1. Involve the staff in planning for department-specific changes and transitions.

2. Announce the changes and then closely supervise staff as they make the transition to the change.

3. Don't push the process; assist workers as the change takes effect.

4. Let the staff manage the change process themselves.

Explanation:

_____

_____

Based on your answers and the definitions in the textbook, what style of leadership do you think you exhibit most often? Describe a personal situation where you have demonstrated this style.

_____

_____

_____

_____

_____

H. Chapter Notes: Ethical Behaviour and Management

Read the fourth section, Ethical Behaviour and Management (pages 217–219), in your textbook, and answer the following questions.

1. List five ways that managers can treat their employees ethically.

_____

_____

_____

_____

2. What policies are typically included in a company's ethical code of conduct?

_____

_____

_____

_____

_____

3. List three ways that a company can minimize environmental damage.

_____

_____

_____

_____

_____

_____

4. List two reasons why implementing environmentally friendly practices is good for a company.

_____

_____

_____

_____

_____

5. How can a company contribute to a charitable organization?

_____

_____

_____

_____

_____

I. Activity: 10 Ways to Be an Environmentally Friendly School

Table 7.1 on page 219 of your textbook lists 10 ways that a business can be environmentally friendly. Work with a partner to create a similar 10-item list for how your school could be greener. Then create a poster that illustrates each strategy. Be sure to mention how these strategies will benefit the environment and lower the school's operating costs. If possible, present the poster to your school's principal.

1. _____

_____

2. _____

_____

3. _____

_____

4. _____

_____

5. _____

_____

6. _____

_____

7. _____

_____

8. _____

_____

9. _____

_____

10. _____

_____

J. Chapter Notes: Teamwork in Companies

Read the fifth section, Teamwork in Companies (pages 220–221), in your textbook, and use the following organizer to help guide your note-taking. Then answer the questions that follow.

1. Provide a definition for each of the six types of teams and give an example of each one.

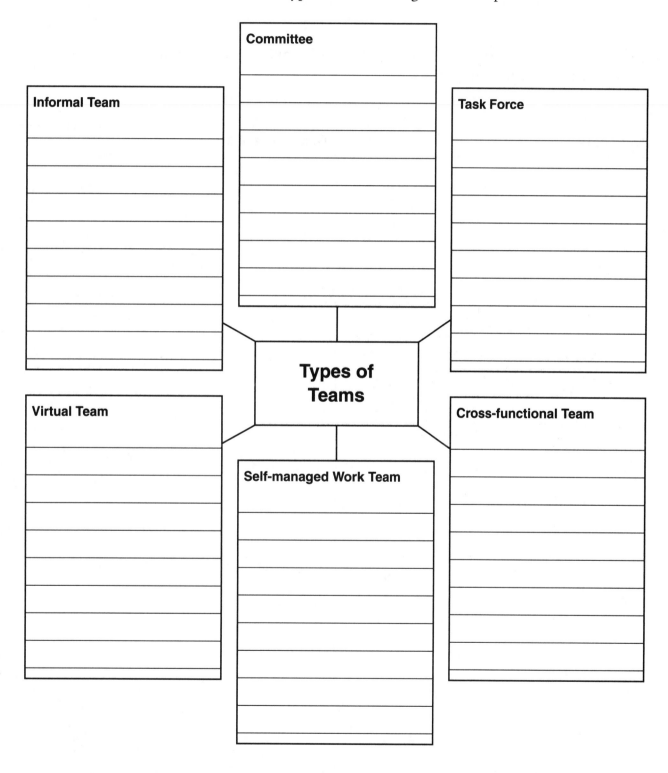

2. Why are teams common in corporations?

_____

_____

_____

_____

_____

3. What are the advantages and disadvantages of teamwork? Write the list in order according to what you believe is most important.

Advantages	Disadvantages

K. Activity: Teamwork Skills

Effective team members need these basic skills:

- Communication and negotiation: the ability to state ideas or questions clearly, listen to others attentively, and resolve disagreements.

- Organization: the ability to stay on task and meet all deadlines.

1. Select a concept from the concept bank and place it under the most appropriate teamwork skill. Do this until all concepts have been placed.

2. Place a checkmark next to each skill that you feel you demonstrate when working with a team.

Concept Bank		
ask questions	define a common goal	give constructive feedback
assign responsibilities	develop a checklist	listen actively
avoid jargon	develop a timeline	list tasks to be completed
be courteous	don't express an opinion as a fact	respond, don't react
compliment another's idea		send reminders when deadlines approach
critique the idea, not the person	don't interrupt	
	explain your reasons	show patience

Teamwork Skills	
Communication and Negotiation	**Organization**

The first Ben & Jerry's Homemade Ice Cream shop opened in 1978 in a renovated gas station in downtown Burlington, Vermont. What began with a $5 investment in an ice cream-making correspondence course has evolved into a company that serves as an ethical role model to others in the corporate world.

The company's altruistic roots were evident from its first anniversary, when every patron walked away with a free ice cream cone. Since these humble beginnings, the company has grown quite active in giving back to the community and in making a commitment to minimize its environmental impact.

The company strives to reduce waste and greenhouse gas emissions, and put into place a plan to lower carbon dioxide emissions by 10 percent between 2002 and 2007. It is also working toward changing its pint-container packing, which will eliminate 1000 tonnes of waste generated from previous packaging material.

At Ben & Jerry's, even the lowest-paid employee earns a salary plus benefits that is above the state average.

The company donates 7.5 percent of pre-tax profits to non-profit organizations through the Ben & Jerry's Foundation. Events held by non-profit organizations in the United States often receive donations of Ben & Jerry's ice cream. Employees participate in community-action projects such as Project Joy, which collects presents, non-perishable food, and employee donations and sends them to Vermont communities facing economic hardship at Christmas time.

Employees of the central office are allowed to take up to 40 hours of paid time off to volunteer with a non-profit organization. In 2005, in response to Hurricane Katrina, Ben & Jerry's sent a team of eight employees to the Gulf Coast to assist with the cleanup efforts.

On the other hand, only Häagen-Dazs costs more than Ben & Jerry's at the grocery store. Some people question the morality of charging so much for ice cream when more than 40 million Americans live below the poverty line and cannot afford such an expenditure. Furthermore, in 2002, the Center for Science in the Public Interest (CSPI) accused Ben & Jerry's of abusing the "All Natural" label by using artificial flavours, hydrogenated oils, and other factory-made substances in their products. Ben & Jerry's official response was that they use a different definition of "all natural" than the CSPI.

Cases such as Ben & Jerry's demonstrate the struggle of attempting socially responsible actions in a complex, global market.

1. In what ways does Ben & Jerry's demonstrate ethical management? Include the company's actions regarding employees, the environment, and the community.

_____

_____

_____

_____

_____

_____

_____

_____

2. In your opinion, do the company's actions regarding pricing and labelling cancel out the good that the company does?

_____

_____

_____

_____

_____

_____

_____

_____

3. Some people believe that companies such as Ben & Jerry's demonstrate ethical management and corporate social responsibility only to gain praise from the media. Do you agree with this statement? Do you believe this type of behaviour is ethical?

_____

_____

_____

_____

_____

_____

_____

_____

M. Review

Business Word Bank		
autocratic	laissez-faire	production
communicating	motivate	purchasing
controlling	organizing	research and development
democratic	planning	

Use the terms given in the word bank to complete the following statements:

1. _____ is the process of setting attainable short-term and long-term goals for a business.

2. _____ means arranging people and activities to meet the plans of a business.

3. A skillful manager learns how to best _____ each employee.

4. A good leader is effective at clearly _____ directions, urgency, corporate values, plans, and goals.

5. Activities involved in _____ include employee discipline, performance appraisals, and budgeting.

6. The _____ manager acquires the raw materials, equipment, supplies, and goods for resale and ensures that they arrive at the right time.

7. Ensuring that the business makes the goods it is supposed to is the work of the _____ manager.

8. The _____ department creates new products or services or makes improvements to existing ones.

9. _____ leaders make decisions without the participation of employees.

10. Allowing employees to do their jobs with little direction from the manager is a characteristic of _____ leadership.

11. Providing opportunities for employees to be involved in decision making is a quality of a(n) _____ leader.

CHAPTER 8: MARKETING

A. Business Vocabulary

In Chapter 8, you'll be introduced to some terms that relate to marketing. Before you begin working with the chapter, browse through the pages and look for the bolded key terms. Use the left-hand side of the chart to write any words you don't immediately understand. Then, when you arrive at the section featuring the word, write its definition in the middle column. Use the last column to note any relevant examples.

Term	Textbook Definition	Examples

B. Chapter Notes: The Role and Impact of Marketing

Read the first section, The Role and Impact of Marketing (pages 229–238), in your textbook, and answer the following questions.

1. What is marketing? Explain its two fundamental roles.

_____

_____

_____

_____

_____

_____

_____

2. Without marketing, not much would get sold. Explain how each group uses marketing, and identify the corresponding area(s) of marketing (research, development, sales, distribution, advertising, or promotion).

Group	How Marketing Is Used	Area of Marketing
Manufacturers		
Importers, wholesalers, and retailers		
Producers		
Stores		
Service businesses		
Non-profit organizations		

3. What is a brand name? Why is it important?

_____

_____

_____

_____

_____

4. What is a logo or trademark? Explain the three types of logos/trademarks and provide an example of each one.

_____

_____

_____

_____

_____

_____

_____

5. How can an effective slogan be beneficial for a brand? Provide an example of an effective slogan.

_____

_____

_____

_____

6. Why would a business want to establish brand identification of a product?

_____

_____

_____

_____

_____

7. What is brand equity? Why is it important to increase the brand equity of a product?

_____

_____

_____

_____

_____

_____

8. How does a style curve influence marketing decisions?

_____

_____

_____

_____

9. Fill out the following the organizer based on the product life cycle. Provide a description of what is happening to the product at each stage of the product life cycle.

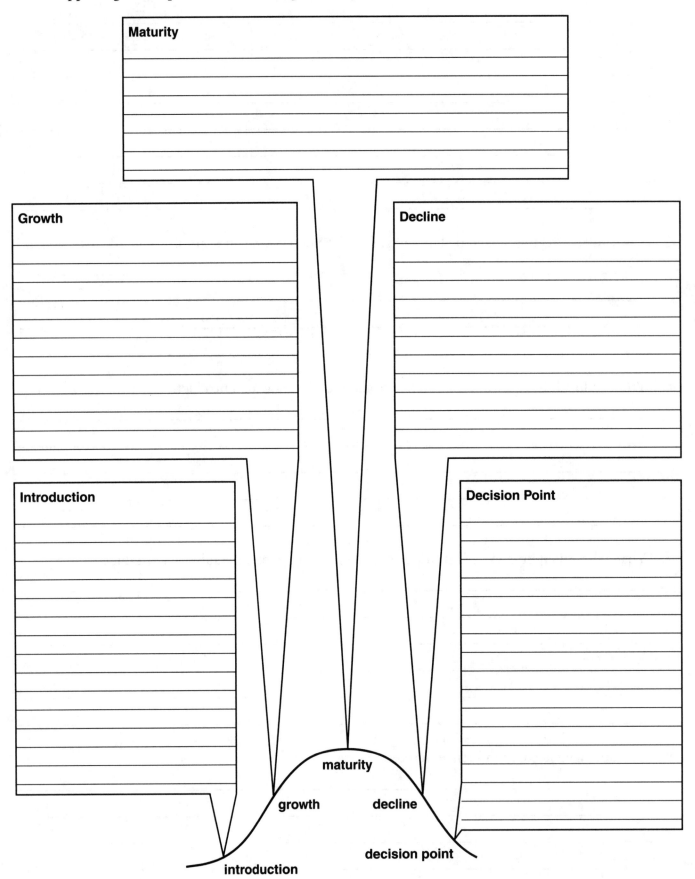

Maturity

Growth

Decline

Introduction

Decision Point

maturity

growth   decline

decision point

introduction

10. List three types of non-traditional product life cycles.

_____

_____

11. Explain the difference between a fad and a trend. Provide an example of each.

_____

_____

_____

_____

12. Explain how fads can either earn or lose a business a lot of money.

_____

_____

_____

_____

13. Explain what it means for a product to have a niche. What types of products are likely to fall into this category?

_____

_____

_____

_____

_____

_____

_____

14. What barriers might prevent competitors from being profitable in a given market?

_____

_____

_____

_____

15. Why is inventory management of seasonal merchandise important for retailers, wholesalers, importers, and manufacturers?

_____

_____

_____

_____

C. Activity: Brand Preference

Effective marketing increases a brand's equity—its value in the marketplace. Marketing develops brand awareness, so that consumers can name the brand as part of a specific category. Better marketing develops brand loyalty, and customers prefer one product over others. The best marketing develops brand insistence, and customers will accept no substitutes.

For each product category listed below, ask yourself the following three questions and record your answers in the chart:

- What brands can I name?
- Which brand do I prefer?
- Will I accept a substitute if the preferred brand is unavailable?

Product Category	Brands I'm Aware Of	Preferred Brand	Substitutes Accepted?
Soft drinks			
Video game consoles			
Chips			
Shampoo			
Blue jeans			
Chewing gum			

1. Working in groups of six, make a list of all the brands that were mentioned in the second column for each category and write them in the second column of the table below.

2. For each category, determine which brand was listed as preferred most often and write it in the third column.

3. For each category, determine which brand is least likely to be accepted as a brand substitute and write it in the fourth column.

Product Category	Brand Awareness	Brand Loyalty	Brand Insistence
Soft drinks			
Video game consoles			
Chips			
Shampoo			
Blue jeans			
Chewing gum			

4. Look at the brands listed in the last column above. What stage in the product life cycle do you think these products are in? Explain why.

_____

_____

_____

_____

5. Why do you think some brands were preferred but did not have brand insistence?

_____

_____

_____

_____

D. Chapter Notes: Marketing Concepts

Read the second section, Marketing Concepts (pages 238–254), in your textbook, and answer the following questions.

1. Describe the four Ps of marketing that product concept marketers are responsible for and the two Cs of marketing examined by market concept marketers.

Product Concept Marketers	
Market Concept Marketers	

2. Explain the importance of the following in good product and service development.

Quality	
Design	
Features	
Benefits	
Product/ service mix	

3. Explain the importance of price to the marketing mix.

_____

_____

_____

_____

_____

_____

_____

4. What is a channel of distribution?

_____

_____

5. Describe each of the channels of distribution.

Channels of Distribution	Definition
Direct Channels	
Indirect Channels	
Importers	
Wholesalers	
Retailers	
Specialty Channels	
Vending machines	
Telemarketing	
Catalogues	
E-commerce	

6. Describe the five types of sales promotion.

Type of Promotion	Description
Coupons	
Contests	
Premiums	
Samples	
Special events	

7. What is the competitive market?

_____

_____

_____

8. Explain the difference between market share and market segment.

_____

_____

_____

9. Explain the two ways that a company can increase its market share.

_____

_____

_____

10. What is the difference between indirect and direct competition? Provide examples.

_____

_____

_____

_____

11. What are demographics? Why do businesses use demographics?

_____

_____

12. Briefly describe each of the following demographic variables.
    a) Age: _____

_____

_____

_____

    b) Gender: _____

_____

_____

_____

    c) Family life cycle: _____

_____

_____

_____

    d) Income level: _____

_____

_____

_____

    e) Ethnicity and culture: _____

_____

_____

_____

13. What is psychographics? Why is it important to marketers?

_____

_____

_____

E. Activity: Direct vs. Indirect Competition

Many products compete for consumers' discretionary income, or the money available to buy things for pleasure. For each set of items, determine whether the products are competing directly or indirectly. If they are direct competition, list the areas in which they are competing, using the four Ps of marketing (product, price, place, and promotion). Your response should include quality, design, features, benefits, the product/service mix, image, and channels of distribution where applicable.

Products	Direct/Indirect Competition	Areas of Direct Competition
Hewlett-Packard vs. Dell computers		
Book vs. movie		
Neutrogena vs. Bioré facial cleanser		
Kleenex vs. Puffs facial tissues		
Concert tickets vs. new outfit		
Aquafresh vs. Arm & Hammer toothpaste		
Hyundai vs. Mercedes		
Cruise vs. all-inclusive resort vacation		

F. Chapter Notes: Advertising

Read the third section, Advertising (pages 255–262), in your textbook, and use the following organizers to guide your note-taking.

1. Explain the four standard rules for creating good print and broadcast advertising.

Advertising Rule	Print Advertising	Broadcast Advertising
Attract attention		
Gain interest		
Build desire		
Get action		

2. Use the Venn diagram to show the similarities and differences between advertising and publicity.

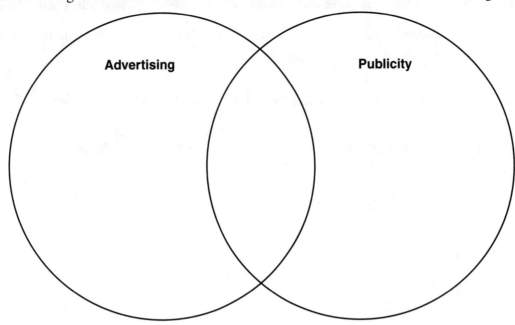

3. Explain each of the following types of advertising.

Type of Advertising	Description
Direct-to-home	
Out-of-home	
Radio	
Television	
Newspaper	
Magazine	
Internet	

4. Use the chart below to compare the eight categories used to evaluate media.

Category	Definition	Media Where it Is Strongest	Media Where it Is Weakest
Reach			
Frequency			
Selectivity			
Durability			
Lead-time			
Mechanical requirements			
Clutter			
Costs			

G. Activity: What Type of Advertising Is Best?

For each situation below, suggest two or more methods of advertising that would be most suitable. Explain your selections.

1. You have just opened a new restaurant in a neighbourhood already heavily populated with eateries. How might you attract customers to your restaurant?

_____

_____

_____

_____

2. You are launching a new brand of sneakers and want to make as many people as possible aware of your brand.

_____

_____

_____

_____

3. The hospital you work for is running a lottery to raise money to build a new wing. You want people in the community to purchase tickets.

_____

_____

_____

_____

4. You would like to increase sales for your brand of golf clubs.

_____

_____

_____

_____

5. You run a small, home-based invitation business and sell your items online. You would like to let people know about your business.

_____

_____

_____

_____

H. Chapter Notes: Marketing Research

Read the fourth section, Marketing Research (pages 262–265), in your textbook, and answer the following questions.

1. What is marketing research? How do marketers determine what type to use?

   _____

   _____

   _____

   _____

   _____

   _____

2. Use the table below to describe each type of market research.

Type of Market Research	Definition
Consumer research	
Market research	
Motivation research	
Pricing research	
Competitive research	
Product research	
Advertising research	

3. What is secondary data? How is it collected?

_____

_____

_____

_____

_____

4. What is primary data? How is it collected?

_____

_____

_____

5. How does test marketing work?

_____

_____

_____

_____

6. What is the purpose of data mining?

_____

_____

_____

_____

_____

7. Explain the difference between closed-ended and open-ended survey questions.

_____

_____

_____

_____

8. What is the purpose of observation in market research?

_____

_____

9. Describe what happens in a focus group.

_____

_____

I. Activity: You Are the Market Researcher

As of March 2007, Ontario cellphone and landline users were able to switch service providers and retain their existing telephone numbers. Imagine that you have been hired by a cellphone company to conduct research into what factors may influence a person to switch providers. The goals of the research are to determine how you can attract customers from other providers while keeping your current customer base.

With a partner, create a 12-question survey that will help you with your research. Your questions should ask for demographic data as well as information on customers' lifestyles, values, needs, and wants. For example, an introductory question might ask, "How long have you owned a cellphone?"

1. _____

2. _____

3. _____

4. _____

5. _____

6. _____

7. _____

8. _____

9. _____

10. _____

11. _____

12. _____

J. Case Study: Fast-Food Biz Wants K-Fed Ad Spiked

Poor Kevin Federline. Even when he tries self-deprecation he fails miserably.

In "Life Comes At You Fast," a commercial for Nationwide Insurance that aired during the Super Bowl in February 2007, the former Mr. Britney Spears—in a role we presume did not require him to flex his limited acting muscles—plays a guy dreaming of being a rapper, only to wake up and realize he's slinging burgers for a living at a dingy fast-food joint.

It all seems harmless enough, but the National Restaurant Association (NRA)—a group that represents 935 000 restaurants in the United States—called on Nationwide not to run the spot, saying it's tired of fast-food workers being portrayed as shiftless losers, Reuters reports.

"An ad such as this is a strong and direct insult to the 12.8 million Americans who work in the restaurant industry," NRA boss Steven Anderson wrote in a letter to the insurance company. "Developing creative concepts that accomplish the marketing strategies for a product should not require denigrating another industry."

But Nationwide—which had to pony up an estimated U.S. $2.5 million for the 30-second spot—defended the ad, saying it was merely a tongue-in-cheek reminder to potential customers about the importance of being prepared for sudden life changes. "The intent of the ad isn't to offend or insult the many fine individuals who work in the restaurant industry," Nationwide spokesman Eric Hardgrove said in a statement. "The focus of the ad is the element of surprise, not the setting of a fast-food restaurant."

1. Why might an ad depicting K-Fed as a fast-food restaurant employee be seen as offensive?

   _____

   _____

   _____

   _____

2. Sometimes ads are designed to create controversy. Why might a company do this?

   _____

   _____

   _____

   _____

3. Create a better ad for Nationwide Insurance, using the "Life Comes At You Fast" slogan. What would happen in this ad?

   _____

   _____

   _____

   _____

K. Review

Business Word Bank		
advertising	fads	price sensitive
brand equity	four Ps of marketing	primary data
brand name	importers	product life cycle
channels of distribution	indirect	psychographics
closed-ended	indirect competition	publicity
competitive	knock-offs	sales promotion
consumer	marketing	secondary data
demographics	marketing research	slogan
direct	market segment	specialty
direct competition	market share	style curve
direct-to-home advertisements	niche	trademark
discretionary income	open-ended	two Cs of marketing
disposable income	out-of-home advertising	wholesalers

Use the terms given in the word bank to complete the following statements:

1. The two roles of _____ are to sell what a business makes and manage a business's brands.

2. A(n) _____ is used to distinguish a company's products from its competitors'.

3. The Golden Arches are a(n) _____ or logo associated with McDonald's.

4. Nike's "Just Do It" is an example of a(n) _____.

5. The value of a brand in the marketplace is known as _____.

6. A brand's equity develops according to its place in the _____ and can be visually demonstrated using a(n) _____.

7. Products that are extremely popular for a short period of time are known as _____. They often spawn imitators known as _____.

8. A product that has a(n) _____ has a dominant section of the market where few competitors will enter.

9. Product, price, place, and promotion are known collectively as the _____.

10. Marketers need to be aware of how _____ their product is before raising or lowering its price.

11. _____ are the paths of ownership that goods follow as they pass from the producer to the consumer. A farmers' market is an example of a(n) _____ channel of distribution. Selling through an intermediary is a(n) _____ channel of distribution. Purchasing from a website is an example of a(n) _____ channel of distribution.

12. _____ bring goods into a country, whereas _____ buy goods from producers or importers and resell them to retailers.

13. _____ encourages consumers to buy a product using coupons, contests, premiums, samples, and special events.

14. The _____ include the _____ market and the _____ market.

15. _____ is the percentage of the market that a company or a brand has, while a(n) _____ is the part of the overall market that has similar characteristics.

16. Products that compete for your money but are not directly related to each other are in _____, while products that are very similar are in _____.

17. The money you have left over after taxes is your _____. The money that is left after paying for basic necessities like food and shelter is your _____.

18. _____ is the study of obvious characteristics like age and gender, whereas _____ is the study of lifestyles.

19. _____ is the paid-for promotion of a business's goods or services, whereas _____ is unpaid promotion.

20. Flyers and catalogues are examples of _____, whereas billboard ads are examples of _____.

21. _____ collects and analyzes information to develop a marketing strategy.

22. Whereas _____ re-analyzes data collected from another source, _____ is collected and analyzed for a specific purpose.

23. "Yes/No" and "Agree/Disagree" are examples of _____ survey questions. _____ survey questions let respondents develop their own answers.

CHAPTER 9: ACCOUNTING

A. Business Vocabulary

In Chapter 9, you'll encounter some terms that relate to accounting. Before you begin working with the chapter, browse through the pages and look for the bolded key terms. Use the left-hand side of the chart to write any words you don't immediately understand. Then, when you arrive at the section featuring the word, write its definition in the middle column. Use the last column to note any relevant examples.

Term	Textbook Definition	Examples

B. Chapter Notes: Basic Accounting Concepts

Read the first section, Basic Accounting Concepts (pages 273–280), in your textbook, and answer the following questions.

1. Explain the function of an accountant in a business.

   _____

   _____

2. Explain the purpose of accounting.

   _____

   _____

   _____

3. What is a transaction? Provide three examples.

   _____

   _____

   _____

4. Explain bookkeeping and double-entry bookkeeping and provide an example.

   _____

   _____

   _____

   _____

5. What are three transactions that can change an individual's chequebook balance?

   _____

   _____

6. Identify two reasons why an individual would use accounting.

   _____

   _____

   _____

7. What is an asset? Would a gift be considered one of your assets? Provide an example.

   _____

   _____

   _____

   _____

8. What is a liability? Provide an example.

_____

_____

_____

9. What is personal equity, or net worth? What is the equation for expressing personal equity or net worth?

_____

_____

10. Explain owner's equity.

_____

_____

11. What equation can you use to determine owner's equity?

_____

12. What equation can you use to determine total assets?

_____

13. Explain how the balance sheet equation can be useful to accountants.

_____

_____

_____

14. What is a balance sheet?

_____

_____

_____

15. Explain the relationship between the cost principle and depreciation.

_____

_____

_____

16. Briefly define accounts receivable, accounts payable, and mortgage payable.

_____

_____

_____

C. Activity: Transactions

In any transaction, at least two things change. If a business uses cash to purchase gas for the company car, the business has less cash and more gas. If the business uses the company credit card to pay for the gas, the business has more gas and an account payable to the credit card company. For each of the transactions listed below, state at least two things that change as a result of the transaction.

1. Purchased cleaning supplies for $300 (cash).

   _____

   _____

2. Paid $500 on a $1500 bank loan.

   _____

   _____

3. Purchased 60 pairs of shoes to sell. Owe the shoe manufacturer $3000.

   _____

   _____

4. Sold 20 pairs of shoes at $100 per pair.

   _____

   _____

5. Paid $1800 rent for the month.

   _____

   _____

6. Bought a new cash register. Owe the business machine company $5000.

   _____

   _____

7. Paid $2500 that was owed to a supplier.

   _____

   _____

8. Invested $5000 cash in the business.

   _____

   _____

D. Chapter Notes: Preparing Financial Statements

Read the second section, Preparing Financial Statements (pages 280–299), in your textbook, and answer the following questions.

1. Identify two groups that may own a business's assets.

   _____

   _____

   _____

2. In the organizer below, outline the five steps in creating a balance sheet. Be sure to include all relevant information.

Step 1:

Step 2:

Step 3:

Step 4:

Step 5:

3. Summarize each of the three types of financial statements.

	Balance Sheet	Income Statement	Statement of Cash Flow
Information provided			
Time period measured			
Usefulness to business			

4. Why do balance sheets have conventions of style? Outline four of these conventions.

_____

_____

_____

_____

_____

_____

5. Explain why creditors, the government, investors, and owners might review a balance sheet.

_____

_____

_____

_____

_____

_____

_____

_____

6. What is revenue?

_____

_____

7. List four examples of expenses. How are expenses used to determine whether a business has achieved a net income or net loss?

_____

_____

_____

8. In the organizer below, outline the four steps in creating an income statement for a service business. Be sure to include all relevant information.

Step 1:

_____

_____

Step 2:

_____

_____

Step 3:

_____

_____

Step 4:

_____

_____

9. What is the matching principle? Why is it important?

_____

_____

_____

_____

10. How are the income statements of a retail business different from that of a service business?

_____

_____

_____

11. State the two income statement equations for a retail business and the equation for cost of goods sold. Explain gross profit and cost of goods sold.

1. _____

2. _____

3. _____

Gross profit: _____

_____

Cost of goods sold: _____

_____

_____

_____

12. Why is good inventory control important for a retail business?

_____

_____

_____

13. Explain why an income statement is prepared before a balance sheet.

_____

_____

_____

_____

14. Provide five examples of sources of cash moving into a business and five examples of expenditures of cash moving out of a business.

_____

_____

_____

_____

15. Why do accountants compare financial data over a set period of time?

_____

_____

_____

_____

_____

_____

E. Activity: Balance Sheet Exercises

Complete a balance sheet for each of the following companies:

1. Prepare a balance sheet for Judy's Boutique, using the following information:

   Cash $3200.00; Gord Lewis owes $475.00; Michael Erb owes $395.00; Inventory $34 000.00; Furniture and Equipment $23 450.00; Building $94 000.00; owed to Titan Wholesale $8420.00; Bank Loan $9460.00; Mortgage $42 000.00.

   Use the basic accounting equation to calculate the equity for owner Judy McCutcheon. Use today's date.

2. Prepare a balance sheet using today's date for Snackbar Haven owned by Anu Persaud. The account balances are as follows:

Bank Loan $8695.25; Supplies $19 742.74; Cash $16 941.19; Mortgage $38 462.91; owed to Lloyd Restaurant Supply $7492.37; Karen's Catering owes $6248.23; Equipment $26 497.36; Building $75 400.00; Furniture $36 481.22. Remember to calculate owner's equity.

F. Activity: Income Statement Exercises

Complete an income statement for each of the following companies:

1. Prepare an income statement for the Law Office of Dewey, Cheetham, and Howe for the month ending December 31, 20___, using the following information:

   Fees $120 000.00; Investment Income $32 000.00; Salaries $12 750.00; Rent $7600.00; Insurance $5000.00; Advertising $3299.00; Office Expenses $2344.00; Transportation Expenses $5460.00; Promotion Expenses $3800.00.

2. Prepare an income statement for the Markville Laundromat for the fiscal year ending June 30, 20___. Select the necessary accounts from the ones listed below.

Cash	$ 1 212.70	Sales	$88 932.29
Accounts Receivable	633.00	Insurance	7 171.00
Laundry Supplies	651.00	Miscellaneous Expense	225.00
Machinery and Equipment	13 900.00	Rent	22 000.00
Trucks	27 050.00	Telephone	574.25
Accounts Payable	1 746.00	Truck Repairs	8 146.90
Bank Loan	23 000.00	Utilities Expense	907.64
A. Ottawa, Capital	21 006.39	Wages	49 908.50

3. Prepare an income statement for retailer UseLess Propane Equipment for the month ending March 31, 20___, using the following information:

Sales $99 000.00; Beginning Inventory $250 000.00; Inventory Purchased $34 500.00; Ending Inventory $198 500.00; Expenses $12 245.00.

G. Case Study: Susan's Music School

Susan runs a music school, where she and her staff teach voice, piano, and violin. She would like to examine the business's finances for the period of 2006 to 2007.

	2007	2006	Increase (+) Decrease (–)
Susan's Music School **Comparative Income Statement** **December 31, 2007 and 2006**			
Revenue			
Sales Revenue	$90 000	$80 000	+ $10 000
Total Revenue	**90 000**	**80 000**	**+ 10 000**
Expenses			
Salaries	38 000	26 000	+ 12 000
Rent	9 600	8 400	+ 1 200
Insurance	2 400	1 600	+ 800
Utilities	1 200	1 000	+ 200
Advertising	1 000	3 000	– 2 000
Supplies	300	500	– 200
Total Expenses	**52 500**	**40 500**	**+ 12 000**
Net Income	**$37 500**	**$39 500**	**$ – 2 000**

1. Carefully examine each income statement. Even though revenue increased by $10 000, net income for 2007 was less than for 2006. What does this tell you about expenses for 2007?

   _____

   _____

2. Which expense experienced the greatest monetary increase in 2007?

   _____

3. Which expense experienced the greatest percentage increase in 2007?

   _____

4. What solutions would you offer to reduce expenses? Explain your answer.

   _____

   _____

   _____

Business Word Bank		
accounting	creditors	maturity date
accounts payable	depreciation	mortgage payable
accounts receivable	double-entry bookkeeping	net profit
asset	expenses	owner's equity
balance sheet	fiscal year	personal equity
balance sheet equation	gross profit	preauthorized payments
bookkeeping	income statement	revenue
cash flow	liabilities	statement of cash flow
cost of goods sold	liquidity	transaction
cost principle	matching principle	

Use the terms given in the word bank to complete the following statements:

1. _____ is the process of recording, analyzing, and interpreting the economic activities of a business.

2. A(n) _____ occurs when something that has value is exchanged for something else that has value.

3. _____ is the method of recording all transactions for a business in a specific format. _____ is based on the principle that each transaction involves two changes.

4. Automatic deductions from your bank account, or _____, can be used to pay recurring items such as utility bills or loan payments.

5. A(n) _____ is something of value that is owned by a person or a business; _____ are debts owed to others.

6. Net worth or _____ is calculated by subtracting liabilities from total assets. _____ is the net worth of a business.

7. Owner's equity and total assets can be determined by using different versions of the _____.

8. A(n) _____ shows the financial position of a business on a certain date.

9. Recording assets at the price the business paid to acquire them is known as the _____.

10. When _____ occurs, an asset loses value over time.

11. Money owed to a business by customers is an asset known as _____; money owed to others by the business is a liability known as _____. The debt owed on a building is a liability known as _____.

12. On a balance sheet, assets are listed in order of _____ or the ease with which an asset can be turned into cash, while liabilities are listed in order by _____, the date by which they must be paid.

13. The people or businesses to whom a business owes money are called the _____ of a business.

14. The _____ measures how much money a business made or lost over a period of time.

15. In an income statement, _____ refers to money or the promise of money received from the sale of goods or services, whereas _____ are things like salaries, advertising, and utilities, which are used to help generate revenue.

16. In order for an income statement to be accurate, accountants use the _____ to match expenses with the revenue generated during the same period.

17. Revenue minus cost of goods sold equals _____.

18. To calculate the _____, add the goods purchased to the opening inventory and then subtract the remaining inventory.

19. A(n) _____ is any 12-month operating period used by a business to measure financial results.

20. _____ is the money that is left after you subtract cost of goods sold and expenses from revenue.

21. _____ is the movement of cash in and out of a business. The _____ reports on the amount of cash coming in and out of a business over a period of time.

CHAPTER 10: CHARACTERISTICS AND SKILLS OF AN ENTREPRENEUR

A. Business Vocabulary

In Chapter 10, you'll learn about the skills and characteristics of a successful entrepreneur. Before you begin working with the chapter, browse through the pages and look for the bolded key terms. Use the left-hand side of the chart below to write any words you don't immediately understand. Then, when you arrive at the section featuring the word, write its definition in the middle column. Use the last column to note any relevant examples.

Term	Textbook Definition	Examples

Read the first section, Entrepreneurial Characteristics (pages 311–315), in your textbook, and use the following organizer to guide your note-taking.

Describe the 10 characteristics of an entrepreneur.

Self-confident

Flexible

Independent

Risk Taker

Hardworking

Perceptive

Entrepreneurial Characteristics

Goal-setting

Persistent

Imaginative

Curious

C. Activity: The Entrepreneur's Diary

It's easy to *say* you can be entrepreneurial, but sometimes actions speak louder than words. Use the chart below to record the times and ways you have shown entrepreneurial characteristics within the past week.

Date:	
Characteristic	**How I Demonstrated This Characteristic**
I was imaginative when I …	
I set goals when I …	
I was perceptive when I …	
I was curious about …	
I took a calculated risk when I …	
I showed persistence when I …	
I worked hard to …	
I was self-confident when I …	
I displayed flexibility when I …	
I was independent when I …	

D. Chapter Notes: Entrepreneurial Skills

Read the second section, Entrepreneurial Skills (pages 315–325), in your textbook, and answer the following questions.

1. Explain why asking the right questions is important for an entrepreneur. How can an initial research question be a springboard for the creation of a new business?

   _____

   _____

   _____

   _____

   _____

   _____

2. Briefly explain how each information source can help an entrepreneur.
   a) Books: _____

   _____

   b) Periodicals: _____

   _____

   c) Indexes and databases: _____

   _____

   d) The Internet: _____

   _____

   e) Consultants: _____

   _____

   f) Professionals: _____

   _____

   g) School: _____

   _____

   _____

3. What is the definition of management for entrepreneurs?

_____

_____

_____

4. Explain the importance of each management skill that an entrepreneur must possess.

   a) Planning: _____

_____

_____

   b) Organizing: _____

_____

_____

   c) Directing: _____

_____

_____

   d) Controlling: _____

_____

_____

5. What is empathy? Provide an example of how an entrepreneur can empathize with an employee.

_____

_____

_____

_____

6. Why is it important to maintain good relationships with suppliers? How can an entrepreneur help maintain a good supplier relationship?

_____

_____

_____

_____

_____

_____

7. Explain the importance of positive customer relationships for an entrepreneur.

_____

_____

Entrepreneurs possess many characteristics. Working with a partner, brainstorm a list of verbs that start with the letters E, N, T, R, P, and U. Then, use each of the letters in the word ENTREPRENEUR to describe an entrepreneurial characteristic.

E _____

_____

N _____

_____

T _____

_____

R _____

_____

E _____

_____

P _____

_____

R _____

_____

E _____

_____

N _____

_____

E _____

_____

U _____

_____

R _____

_____

F. Chapter Notes: Some Canadian Entrepreneurs

Read the third section, Some Canadian Entrepreneurs (pages 325–329), in your textbook, and take notes on the three Canadian entrepreneurs. Describe who they are, how they became entrepreneurs, and what they have accomplished as entrepreneurs.

Jimmy Pattison:

_____

_____

_____

_____

_____

_____

Vickie Kerr:

_____

_____

_____

_____

_____

_____

_____

_____

David Tuccaro:

_____

_____

_____

_____

_____

_____

_____

_____

_____

G. Activity: The Greatest Canadian Entrepreneur

Every year, the Canadian Marketing Association holds a vote for the greatest Canadian entrepreneur. Use the Canadian entrepreneur profiles found at the beginning of Chapters 1–11 of your textbook to conduct your own vote. List each Canadian entrepreneur profiled, the name of his or her business, and a short description of what the business does. In groups of three or four, come up with a list of criteria that you will use to judge each entrepreneur and decide on a winner. Explain your choice.

Entrepreneur(s)	Business Name	Brief Description of Business

Criteria for best entrepreneur:

1. _____

2. _____

3. _____

Greatest Canadian entrepreneur: _____

Reasons this entrepreneur is the greatest: _____

_____

_____

H. Chapter Notes: Venture Evaluation Criteria

Read the fourth section, Venture Evaluation Criteria (pages 329–330), in your textbook, and answer the following questions.

1. Describe how each factor can be used to help you determine whether a venture is feasible:
   a) Financing: _____

   _____

   b) Location: _____

   _____

   c) Licenses and permits: _____

   _____

   d) Suppliers: _____

   _____

   e) Staff: _____

   _____

2. List five questions an entrepreneur should ask regarding marketability.
   1. _____

   _____

   2. _____

   _____

   3. _____

   _____

   4. _____

   _____

   5. _____

   _____

3. What can an entrepreneur do to measure profitability?

   _____

   _____

   _____

   _____

   _____

   _____

I. Activity: Evaluating a Venture

1. Before starting a venture, an entrepreneur needs to evaluate his or her idea against several criteria. In the table below, determine whether the action listed relates to the feasibility, marketability, or profitability of a venture by placing an x in the appropriate box.

Action	Feasibility	Marketability	Profitability
Determining whether your product, service, or charity is competitively priced			
Describing your staffing needs			
Preparing an income statement that lists projected revenue and foreseeable expenses			
Outlining the details of your location choice			
Listing the source of capital with details			
Determining who your competition is			
Making sure that your revenue exceeds your costs			
Determining if your target market wants the product			
Making a list of suppliers			
Determining where, when, and how you will obtain any necessary licences and permits			
Determining how long the venture will last			
Determining what makes your product, service, or charity unique			

2. Which action do you think is most crucial? Explain your answer.

_____

_____

_____

_____

_____

_____

J. Case Study: Faith Seekings Design

You can be the most talented person on the planet, but it doesn't mean you know how to run a business. Building a business requires many diverse skills, and it's nearly impossible for one person to know how to do everything. "You have to be humble enough to admit you can learn from other people," comments entrepreneur Faith Seekings.

Seekings owns a growing graphic design agency called Faith Seekings Design. Her team—which includes Candy, the company dog—operates from her studio near St. Lawrence Market in downtown Toronto. Seekings' design services span identity creation, printed collateral materials, tradeshow booths, website development, and advertising campaigns. "We help our clients to truly relate to their market, not just look pretty," she says.

Seekings got some support from successful people right at the beginning of her entrepreneurial career. "I was laid off from my previous job and landed some freelance work," she recalls. "After a few days as a freelancer, my mentor offered to let me use his office space and equipment to start building my own business. He didn't want anything for expenses until I started to make some money."

While she knew she had a talent for graphic design, Seekings also knew she needed to learn from other people how to build a successful business. "I have a mentor, a professional business coach, and I belong to several business organizations where I get to learn from a wide range of skilled people," she says.

Seekings is chair of Ryze Toronto, a member of Junior Chamber International, and most recently accepted a volunteer position as the Director of Marketing for the Canadian Association of Women Executives and Entrepreneurs (CAWEE). She also belongs to an informal peer mentoring group where members share ideas and encourage each other.

With two full-time employees and a growing list of subcontractors and suppliers, Seekings also looks for help from her own team to grow her business. "You've got to embrace the knowledge of people around you," she says. "I hire very talented people and learn from them every day."

1. How did Faith Seekings become an entrepreneur?

   _____

   _____

   _____

   _____

   _____

2. Why was it important for her to seek guidance from others? From whom did she seek it?

   _____

   _____

   _____

   _____

   _____

Business Word Bank		
database	Listserv	private-label
empathy	marketability	profitability
entrepreneur	periodical index	skills
feasibility		

Use the terms given in the word bank to complete the following statements:

1. A(n) _____ is a person who takes risks and starts a venture to solve a problem or take advantage of an opportunity.

2. Cott is a Canadian _____ bottler that makes soft drinks for brands such as President's Choice and Master Choice.

3. A professional hockey player should have strong athletic _____.

4. Entrepreneurs can find articles about the market they want to enter by using a(n) _____, which lists all the articles published about specific topics over a particular period of time.

5. A(n) _____ is a list of information organized by category.

6. When researching a new venture, an entrepreneur may wish to subscribe to a(n) _____ to receive information by e-mail.

7. Entrepreneurs need _____ to help understand what motivates their employees.

8. When evaluating a venture, it is important to evaluate the _____ of an idea to see if it can actually be implemented.

9. Evaluating the _____ of an idea helps an entrepreneur determine the product's place in the market.

10. _____ is the measure of whether revenue exceeds costs.

CHAPTER 11: INVENTION AND INNOVATION

A. Business Vocabulary

In Chapter 11, you'll encounter some terms related to invention and innovation. Before you begin working with the chapter, browse through the pages and look for the bolded key terms. Use the left-hand side of the chart below to write any words you don't immediately understand. Then, when you arrive at the section featuring the word, write its definition in the middle column. Use the last column to note any relevant examples.

Term	Textbook Definition	Examples

Read the first section, Entrepreneurial Opportunities (pages 337–343), in your textbook, and use the following organizer to guide your note-taking. Then answer the questions that follow.

1. Use the Venn diagram to compare idea-driven and market-driven enterprises.

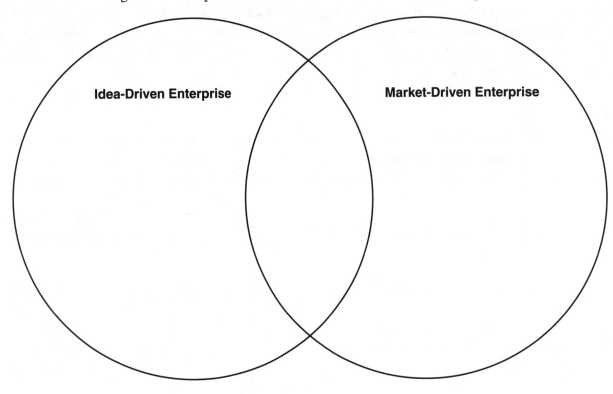

Idea-Driven Enterprise

Market-Driven Enterprise

2. Where can entrepreneurs learn the necessary marketing and technical skills for their inventions? Where can they look for help if they don't want to learn these skills?

_____

_____

_____

_____

_____

_____

_____

_____

3. List three business channels through which an idea person can meet a marketing person.

_____

_____

4. What is a feasible venture? What kind of research will help determine the feasibility of a venture?

_____

_____

_____

_____

_____

_____

_____

5. Describe the type of person who would be interested in each venture category.
   a) Manufacturing: _____

   _____

   b) Importing or wholesaling: _____

   _____

   c) Retail sales: _____

   _____

   d) Service (other than retail): _____

   _____

6. What is segmenting? How does it relate to product mapping?

   _____

   _____

   _____

   _____

   _____

   _____

7. What type of question should an entrepreneur keep in mind as he or she conducts segmenting and product or service mapping? Provide two examples.

   _____

   _____

   _____

   _____

   _____

   _____

C. Activity: Researching a Market

An entrepreneur investigating a market conducts segmenting and creates a product or service map. With a partner, select a product or service you are interested in, and determine its market segment. Then create a product or service map outlining the characteristics of similar items already available in the market. Use page 342 of your textbook as a guide.

Product/service: _____

Market segment: _____

D. Chapter Notes: Some Canadian Inventions

Read the second section, Some Canadian Inventions (pages 343–345), in your textbook, and complete the Canadian invention crossword.

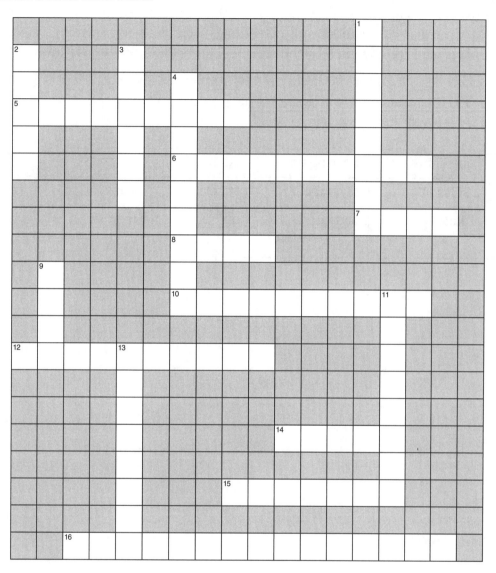

Across

5. This type of paper is inexpensive.
6. Players win this game by defining obscure words.
7. Jacques Plante invented the goalie _____.
8. It's fun to watch movies on _____ screens.
10. This vehicle travels across snow and ice.
12. James Naismith invented this sport.
14. Dr. John A. _____ invented the cardiac pacemaker.
15. A dish of fries, gravy, and cheese curds.
16. _____ _____ invented Standard Time.

Down

1. The _____ is used for construction and repair during space exploration.
2. Canada's Aboriginal peoples invented this watercraft.
3. Your pants might not stay up without this.
4. Dr. Banting and Dr. Best's invention of insulin is a life-saving drug for _____.
9. James Gosling invented _____.
11. This is one of Canada's national sports.
13. Scientists can "see" small particles thanks to the _____ microscope.

E. Activity: Create Your Own Invention

Through his cartoons, which depict the most elaborate and ridiculous devices to accomplish the most mundane tasks, Rube Goldberg's "Inventions" have become synonymous with any maximum effort to achieve minimal results. His ingenious drawings follow their own impeccable logic, demonstrating that the unnecessary can also be the mother of invention—often with comic results. Goldberg's audience includes fans who are intrigued by the creativity and possibility of invention.

There are many examples of Goldberg devices on the Internet. Use a search engine to help find some of these websites. Then, create your own Goldberg device cartoon in the space provided, using any of these 18 items, plus up to three of your own.

cat	ice cubes	bowling ball	matchbook	clock	hornets' nest
cannon	scissors	springboard	bucket	hose	kettle
balloon	paddle	candle	dog	magnet	umbrella

F. Chapter Notes: Taking the Next Step

Read the third section, Taking the Next Step (pages 346–349), in your textbook, and answer the following questions.

1. Explain the difference between a patent and a copyright.

   _____

   _____

   _____

2. What is licensing? Why is it one of the easiest ways to capitalize on an invention or innovation?

   _____

   _____

   _____

   _____

3. Explain why a company would license an idea, an image, or a name. Provide an example.

   _____

   _____

   _____

4. What is a franchise agreement? Who is the entrepreneur in this situation?

   _____

   _____

   _____

5. Why would an inventor form a partnership with an established business or financial investor?

   _____

   _____

   _____

   _____

6. Why would an inventor sell the rights to his or her invention?

   _____

   _____

   _____

   _____

   _____

G. Activity: Licensing

Licensing agreements can involve products, ideas, an image, or a name. You have probably seen lots of merchandise featuring The Simpsons, such as puzzles, board games, and plush toys. Fill out the chart below by identifying at least three licensed characters, teams, or names for each category and list as many products as you can think of that are available because of this license. Try to come up with different products for each category.

Type of Character/Team/Name	Character/Team/Name Examples	Products Based on the Character/Team/Name
Book characters		
Movie characters		
TV characters		
Sports figures		
Celebrities		
Sports teams		
Bands		

H. Chapter Notes: The Impact of Innovation

Read the fourth section, The Impact of Innovation (pages 350–356), in your textbook, and answer the following questions.

1. What is the difference between an invention and an innovation?

   _____

   _____

   _____

2. Use the graphic organizer to explain how innovative changes affect inventions. Provide an example of each type of change.

Type of Change	Description of Change	Example
Changing how a product is used		
Changing the package		
Changing the marketing strategy		
Changing the distribution process		
Changing the design		
Changing the manufacturing process		

I. Activity: Improving Products

For each type of innovation, select a product that you think could be improved using this type of innovation. Describe how you would improve the product, outlining your reasons for this change (for example, changing the packaging of potato chips from bags to tubes to preserve freshness.)

Type of Innovation	Product	Method of Improvement	Reasons for Innovation
Use			
Packaging			
Marketing strategies			
Distribution channels			
Design			
Manufacturing process			

J. Case Study: Remembering the MCM/70

Over 30 years ago, Canada secured a place in computing history. In 1973, a small Toronto company, Micro Computer Machines Inc. owned by Mers Kutt, developed a new machine: the MCM/70. Small and powerful, the MCM/70 was one of the first portable, personal computers. It was also one of the first computers to use a microprocessor. Experts say it deserves a place in digital history because it brought computers to a wider audience.

Kutt did an awful lot with very little, computer historians say, given the state of technology back then. "It was just amazing what they were able to do," said Lee Courtney, an artifact coordinator at the Computer History Museum in Mountain View, Calif. "They built an incredible system with very primitive hardware."

The MCM/70 looks a bit like an old-fashioned answering machine with a built-in keyboard. Designed in a time before floppy disks, the MCM/70 used automated tape drives to store information and had only a small fraction of the computer memory used on a standard computer today. It was coveted by computer programmers, accountants, and insurance agents for its power, small size, and reasonable price tag.

Kutt came up with the concept for the MCM/70 while working at Queen's University. Part of his job was to get more of the professors using computers. At the time, people would have to line up with punch cards and wait to use one of the university's large mainframes.

Long before the famous Apple 1 PC, which debuted in 1976, Kutt saw the value of a smaller, personal system. He wanted to make a computer for each person, small enough to fit in a regular office. "I thought, What if each person had their own computer with their own processor? They wouldn't have to share the processing power," Kutt said. To do this, Kutt knew he'd need a microprocessor. This might seem obvious today, but in 1973 microprocessors were rather novel. Most computers were still using scores of computer chips to do what today can be done on a single microchip and, consequently, these machines could take up whole rooms.

Kutt wanted something that could fit in a suitcase, so he built around Intel Corp.'s 8008 microprocessor. Weighing 20 pounds, the MCM/70 wasn't as light as today's laptops. But it was much more portable than other minicomputers of the period, which often had to be wheeled around on carts.

It packed a fair bit of power for such a small computer. It could solve complex mathematical problems and, when the work was done, run simple video games. Computer collector Stan Sieler of Cupertino, Calif., wants to add an MCM/70 to his collection because he considers it "an incredible achievement" for the time. He remembers seeing one in 1975 and was impressed by the power and the price of the machine, which ran the complex programming language APL. "I was using a million-dollar machine to do APL, and this was a $4500 machine that could do the same thing," Sieler said.

Kutt said thousands were sold worldwide. But MCM never did achieve the status of such competitors as International Business Machines Corp. and Apple Computer Inc. In fact, the MCM/70 could be described as the Avro Arrow of computing history. It was truly ahead of its time and showed lots of promise, but never quite took off because, at least in part, it was made in Canada, far from computing's heartland. Courtney said that, in the 1970s, the "ecosystem" needed to support a high-tech company likely couldn't be found outside California. Kutt agrees, adding that few Canadians in finance and management could wrap their heads around the idea.

1. How did the MCM/70 revolutionize personal computing?

_____

_____

_____

_____

_____

_____

_____

_____

_____

2. Micro Computer Machines went out of business in the early 1980s. How is it possible that a business with a great idea might not survive?

_____

_____

_____

_____

_____

_____

_____

_____

_____

3. How is it possible that the inventor of a product as popular as the personal computer is neither famous nor wealthy as a result?

_____

_____

_____

_____

_____

_____

_____

_____

K. Review

Business Word Bank		
copyright	innovation	patent
feasible venture	invention	product mapping
franchise agreement	licensing	royalty
idea-driven enterprise	market-driven enterprise	venture capital markets

Use the terms given in the word bank to complete the following statements:

1. A(n) _____ is an enterprise created as a result of an invention or innovation.

2. If you start with a customer base and develop a product to meet the customers' needs and wants, you are creating a(n) _____.

3. A(n) _____ has the potential to succeed because the entrepreneur has set reasonable goals, and there is both a market and a need for the product or service.

4. _____ lets an entrepreneur visualize all the features of the products in a particular market segment.

5. A(n) _____ is a process or product that does something that has never been done before.

6. A(n) _____ gives an inventor the sole right to make, use, or sell an invention for a set period of time, preventing others from using it without permission.

7. _____ holders have the exclusive right to publish, produce, sell, or distribute works of literature, music, art, and software.

8. _____ an invention allows a business to use an invention for a fee.

9. A(n) _____ is a fee paid to the owner of a patent or copyright.

10. A company can license the rights to use its name and procedures to another business by entering into a(n) _____.

11. _____ bring inventors and investors together.

12. No one really invented colour television, it was a(n) _____.

CHAPTER 12: INCOME MANAGEMENT

A. Business Vocabulary

In Chapter 12, you'll encounter some terms related to income management. Before you begin working with the chapter, browse through the pages and look for the bolded key terms. Use the left-hand side of the chart to write any words you don't immediately understand. Then, when you arrive at the section featuring the word, write its definition in the middle column. Use the last column to note any relevant examples.

Term	Textbook Definition	Examples

B. Chapter Notes: What Is Money?

Read the first section, What Is Money? (pages 365–367), in your textbook, and answer the following questions.

1. Why is money so important in our economy?

   _____

   _____

2. What is legal tender? Briefly describe two types of legal tender.

   _____

   _____

3. Why are cheques and credit cards not considered legal tender?

   _____

   _____

4. Who decides when new bank notes will be issued? Provide two possible reasons why bank notes may be changed.

   _____

   _____

5. Canadian bank notes have special features to discourage counterfeiting (producing fake money). Describe the security features on a $5 bill.

Security Feature	Description
Holographic stripe	
Watermark portrait	
See-through numbers	
Security thread	

6. What factors affect the purchasing power of money? How is purchasing power measured?

   _____

   _____

   _____

   _____

C. Activity: Consumer Purchasing Power

Money's true value is in its purchasing power. Because of inflation, prices tend to rise and the dollar buys less from one year to the next.

1. The chart below looks at your purchasing power and what happens to that power over time as a result of 2.5 percent inflation. Pretend that that you have won a lottery that pays $50 000.00 a year for life. Your winnings of $50 000.00 and purchasing power are equal at the beginning of the first year. The first two calculations have been done for you.

Year	Purchasing Power at the Beginning of the Year	Inflation (%)	Decline in Purchasing Power at the End of the Year
0	$50 000.00	n/a	n/a
1	$50 000.00	2.5	$1 250.00
2	$48 750.00	2.5	
3		2.5	
4		2.5	
5		2.5	
6		2.5	
7		2.5	
8		2.5	

2. How much has your purchasing power decreased between the beginning of year 0 and the end of year 8? (Don't forget to subtract the decline from your year 8 purchasing power.)

_____

_____

_____

_____

_____

3. Why would inflation be hard on people with fixed incomes?

_____

_____

_____

_____

_____

_____

_____

D. Chapter Notes: What Is Income?

Read the second section, What Is Income? (pages 368–370), in your textbook, and answer the following questions.

1. What is income?

_____

_____

2. How do most people earn their income? What other sources of income exist?

_____

_____

_____

3. Use the organizer below to make notes about gross income, disposable income, and discretionary income.

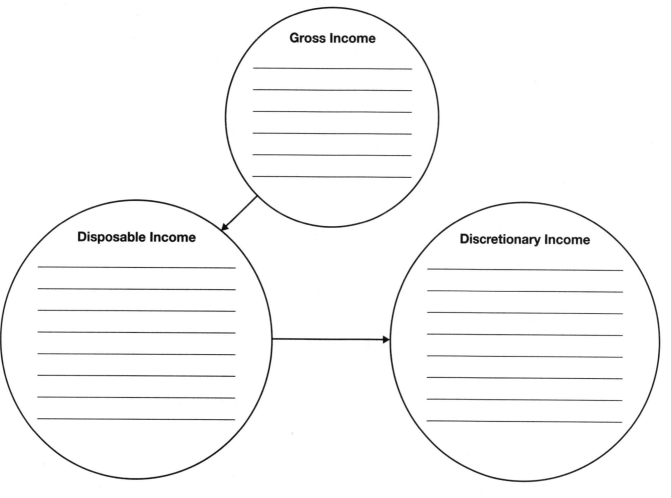

4. What factors decrease how much income tax you will need to pay?

_____

_____

E. Activity: Calculating Income

Gross income is the total amount of income received before deductions. Disposable income is the amount of income left after deductions; it is used to pay for basic necessities such as food, shelter, and clothing. Discretionary income is the amount of income left after necessities have been paid for, and it can be used to buy things for pleasure, such as a vacation. Fill in the spaces in the chart by determining the missing calculation. The first row has been completed for you.

Gross Income (monthly)	Deductions	Disposable Income	Cost of Necessities	Discretionary Income
$ 2 600.00	$ 260.00	$2 340.00	$1 875.93	$ 464.07
$ 4 750.00	$1 750.00		$1 792.16	
	$ 128.00	$1 472.00		$ 319.27
$ 800.00		$ 760.00	$ 175.00	
$ 2 975.00	$ 800.00		$ 900.00	
$ 6 000.00		$3 900.00		$1 400.00
	$1 200.00	$2 975.00	$2 283.37	
$ 3 100.00		$2 325.00	$2 324.72	
$ 5 200.00		$3 640.00		$ 463.27
$10 000.00	$4 000.00		$3 259.12	
	$ 91.60	$1 053.40		$ 753.40

F. Chapter Notes: Managing Money for Personal Use

Read the third section, Managing Money for Personal Use (pages 370–374), in your textbook, and answer the following questions.

1. What is money management?

_____

_____

_____

_____

2. Explain how each factor influences consumer buying decisions.

Factor	How it Influences Purchases
Income	
Price	
Status	
Trends	
Customs	
Lifestyle advertising	

G. Activity: Why Did You Buy?

Six key factors influence consumer buying decisions: income, price, status, current trends, customs and habits, and promotion. Think about the last 10 purchases you made, and determine which of these factors influenced your product or service choice. Explain how each factor affected your decision.

Product/Service Purchased	Factors Influencing Purchase	How Factors Had an Influence

H. Chapter Notes: Spending Money

Read the fourth section, Spending Money (pages 374–377), in your textbook, and answer the following questions.

1. What is comparison shopping? What are the advantages of comparison shopping?

_____

_____

_____

_____

_____

2. In the organizer below, describe each factor to be considered when comparison shopping.

Comparison Factor(s)	Description
Price and quality	
Features	
Services	

3. How might planning and comparing play a role in comparison shopping?

_____

_____

_____

_____

_____

I. Activity: Comparison Shopping

Wise consumers shop around before making a purchase. They compare price, quality, and product features at various retailers. They also take into consideration the services offered by the retailer.

1. Choose a product that you might like to purchase, either now or sometime in the future. Then, comparison shop for this product by visiting three different retailers (either stores or online businesses) that carry the product. Evaluate each retailer on the following criteria: price, quality, features, and service.

Item:	Retailer 1:	Retailer 2:	Retailer 3:
Price			
Quality			
Features			
Service			

2. From which retailer would you purchase the item? Explain your decision by discussing price, quality, features, and service.

_____

_____

_____

_____

_____

_____

_____

J. Chapter Notes: When to Buy

Read the fifth section, When to Buy (pages 378–380), in your textbook, and answer the following questions.

1. Explain why stores hold clearance sales.

   _____

   _____

   _____

   _____

2. Explain why retailers and manufacturers might hold promotional sales.

   _____

   _____

   _____

   _____

   _____

3. What is second-hand shopping? What are the advantages and disadvantages of second-hand shopping?

   _____

   _____

   _____

   _____

   _____

   _____

   _____

4. Provide four reasons why you should avoid impulse buying.

   _____

   _____

   _____

   _____

   _____

   _____

K. Activity: Impulse Buying

1. Most people have, at some time, made a purchase on impulse. List the last 10 items you purchased, and determine whether each was bought on impulse.

Item	Retailer	Reason Purchased	Was the purchase an impulse buy?

2. Work with a partner to come up with five strategies to help you avoid impulse buying.

   1. _____

   2. _____

   3. _____

   4. _____

   5. _____

L. Chapter Notes: Budgeting

Read the sixth section, Budgeting (pages 380–385), in your textbook, and answer the following questions.

1. What is a budget? How does a budget help you?

_____

_____

2. How do families and businesses each use a budget?

_____

_____

3. What role do personal goals play in budgeting?

_____

_____

_____

_____

4. Outline the steps in developing a budget.

Step	Description
1	
2	
3	
4	

5. Why is it important to review your expenses on a regular basis?

_____

_____

6. What might you do if you are having trouble achieving savings goals despite trimming expenses?

_____

_____

M. Activity: Preparing a Personal Budget

A budget can help you make wise financial decisions and help you manage your money. Budgeting is a skill you can use your entire life; even though you're young, it is never too soon to learn how to make and stick to a budget.

1. Consider the income you receive through your allowance or part-time job and use this to make a daily, weekly, or monthly budget. For each budget component, determine how your money will be spent. You can add an additional component if necessary. Once you have completed this for each component, determine what percentage of your income should be allotted to it.

Budget Component	Where My Money Will Go	Percentage of Budget
Savings		
Post-secondary savings		
Donations		
Planned spending		
Mad money		

2. Create a pie chart like the one on page 381 of your textbook to illustrate how you will spend your money.

Budgeting My Income

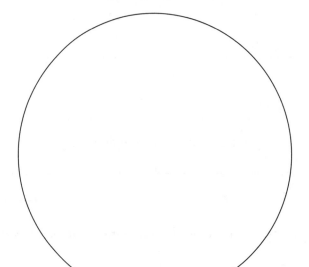

N. Chapter Notes: Managing Money for Business Use

Read the seventh section, Managing Money for Business Use (pages 385–389), in your textbook, and answer the following questions.

1. Discuss three differences between budgeting for a business and budgeting for personal use.

   _____

   _____

   _____

   _____

   _____

2. Briefly describe each type of business income.
   a) Revenue: _____

   _____

   b) Gross income: _____

   _____

   c) Net income: _____

   _____

3. Explain why budgets are important in business.

   _____

   _____

4. Briefly describe each type of business budget.
   a) Start-up budget: _____

   _____

   b) Operating budget: _____

   _____

5. What kinds of goals do businesses set?

   _____

   _____

6. Outline the steps in preparing a business budget.
   Step 1: _____
   Step 2: _____
   Step 3: _____
   Step 4: _____

O. Activity: Setting Prices

Imagine that you are a street vendor of hot dogs. It is a new year and you must determine the hot dog price for the upcoming year. Calculate the daily and monthly revenue, total expenses, and net income for each hot dog price, taking into account fixed and variable costs. Assume there are 30 days in a month. Then determine the price you would charge to earn a maximum profit.

Hot Dog Price	Hot Dogs Sold per Day	Daily Revenue	Monthly Revenue	Monthly Variable Expenses	Monthly Fixed Expenses	Total Costs	Net Profit
$1.25	130			$97.50	$3000.00		
$1.50	120			$90.00	$3000.00		
$1.75	110			$82.50	$3000.00		
$2.00	100			$75.00	$3000.00		
$2.25	90			$67.50	$3000.00		
$2.50	80			$60.00	$3000.00		
$2.75	70			$52.50	$3000.00		
$3.00	60			$45.00	$3000.00		
$3.25	50			$37.50	$3000.00		
$3.50	40			$30.00	$3000.00		

Price I would charge: _____

_____

P. Case Study: The Millers' Budget

Nancy and Shawn Miller are a newly married couple in their early 30s. They are currently renting a one-bedroom apartment in the city but would like to purchase a two-bedroom condominium within the next two years. Their combined gross annual income is $96 000. Each month, they pay $700 in wedding debt and $610 for student loans. Rent is $1200 and includes utilities. Their monthly transit passes cost $200. They spend $520 each month on groceries and an additional $275 for cable, Internet, and telephone. Approximately $250 is spent every month on clothing. They like to have about $350 per week in discretionary income for leisure and miscellaneous expenses, such as movies, books, and CDs. They would like to save $15 000 over the next two years for a down payment. Create a monthly budget for Nancy and Shawn. Assume tax deductions of 30 percent.

Monthly Budget

1. How much money is left over at the end of the month? Is this enough to save $15 000 in two years?

   _____

   _____

2. How much would they have to save each month to achieve their $15 000 goal within two years?

   _____

3. How would you recommend Shawn and Nancy trim their budget in order to have more money for savings?

   _____

   _____

   _____

Business Word Bank		
bank notes	fixed expenses	promotional sales
budget	gross income	second-hand shopping
clearance sales	impulse buying	start-up budget
conspicuous consumption	income	variable expenses
Consumer Price Index	legal tender	warranty
counterfeiting	operating budget	

Use the terms given in the word bank to complete the following statements:

1. The two main forms of _____ are coins and Bank of Canada _____.

2. _____ is the production of fake money.

3. The _____ measures the purchasing power of money on a monthly basis.

4. Money received by an individual or business from various sources is known as _____. _____ is the total amount of income received by a person.

5. _____ occurs when purchases are made in order to impress others.

6. A(n) _____ is a promise that a product is of a certain quality.

7. Stores hold _____ to sell merchandise at a reduced price to make room for the next season's goods. _____ can be held to draw in new customers.

8. _____ saves you money while supporting the three Rs of waste management.

9. _____ occurs when you buy something without thinking first.

10. A plan for how income will be spent is known as a(n) _____.

11. In a budget, _____ occur regularly and cannot be adjusted; _____ differ from one month to another.

12. A(n) _____ shows the money needed to open a business; a(n) _____ sets out the ongoing revenues and expenses of a company.

CHAPTER 13: BANKING

A. Business Vocabulary

In Chapter 13, you'll encounter some terms related to banking. Before you begin working with the chapter, browse through the pages and look for the bolded key terms. Use the left-hand side of the chart below to write any words you don't immediately understand. Then, when you arrive at the section featuring the word, write its definition in the middle column. Use the last column to note any relevant examples.

Term	Textbook Definition	Examples

B. Chapter Notes: The Need for Financial Institutions

Read the first section, The Need for Financial Institutions (pages 396–402), in your textbook, and answer the following questions.

1. Describe three ways banks earn profits.

   _____

   _____

   _____

2. What is the *Bank Act*?

   _____

   _____

   _____

   _____

3. Briefly define the characteristics of the three classes of Canadian banks, and provide two examples of each.

Class	Description
Schedule I banks	
Schedule II banks	
Schedule III banks	

4. List the five advantages of branch banking.

   1. _____

   _____

   2. _____

   _____

   3. _____

   _____

   4. _____

   _____

   5. _____

   _____

5. List three ways that branch banking is changing.

   1. _____

   _____

   2. _____

   _____

   3. _____

   _____

6. What is the function of the Bank of Canada?

   _____

   _____

   _____

   _____

7. What are the consequences of rising and falling interest rates?

   _____

   _____

   _____

   _____

The chart and graph below show the net profits for each of the Big Five banks in Canada in 2005 and 2006 in millions of dollars.

Big Five Bank Earnings 2005–2006 (in millions of dollars)		
	2005	**2006**
BMO	2400	2663
CIBC	(32)	2646
RBC	3387	4728
Scotiabank	3209	3579
TD	2229	4603

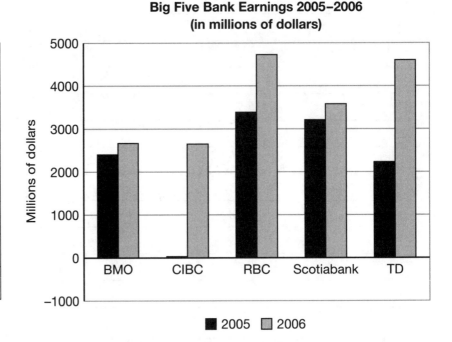

1. Rank the banks from most profitable to least profitable in 2005 and 2006.

2005	2006
1.	1.
2.	2.
3.	3.
4.	4.
5.	5.

2. Which bank's earnings had the greatest dollar increase from 2005 to 2006?

_____

_____

3. Banks earn revenue through service fees, interest on loans, and investments. What are two factors that may cause a bank to not turn a profit?

_____

_____

_____

_____

D. Chapter Notes: Other Financial Institutions

Read the second section, Other Financial Institutions (pages 402–405), in your textbook, and use the following organizer to help guide your note-taking.

Describe the three other financial institutions available in Canada.

Financial Institution	Description
Trust companies	
Caisses populaires and credit unions	
Insurance companies	

E. Activity: Comparing Financial Institutions

1. Although chartered banks are the most common type of financial institution in Canada, they are not the only type. Compare the different types of financial institutions by placing an x in the column(s) in which each statement applies.

	Chartered Banks	Trust Companies	Caisses Populaires and Credit Unions
Organized and owned by groups of people			
Offer personal loans			
Offer lines of credit			
Depositors' accounts are protected by the CDIC			
Regulated by the *Bank Act*			
Offer mortgages			
Depositors' accounts are protected by provincial legislation			
Offer commercial loans			
Borrowing amounts are determined by a committee of members			
Services are provided only to members and their families			
Maintain trust accounts for charitable organizations and minors			
Are not-for-profit organizations			

2. Based on the information above, which type of financial institution do you think you would seek out if you were to open a new bank account? Explain.

_____

_____

_____

F. Chapter Notes: About Accounts

Read the third section, About Accounts (pages 405–409), in your textbook, and answer the following questions.

1. How is a joint account different from a single-person account?

   _____

   _____

   _____

2. When opening an account, what kind of information may a financial institution ask you to provide?

   _____

   _____

   _____

3. List the five pieces of acceptable identification for opening a new bank account. What features must this identification contain?

   _____

   _____

   _____

4. What is a signature card? Why is it necessary?

   _____

   _____

   _____

5. What is an account statement?

   _____

   _____

   _____

6. What is an automated banking machine (ABM) used for? What is required in order to use an ABM?

   _____

   _____

   _____

   _____

   _____

G. Activity: ABM Security

Automated banking machines (ABMs) are a convenient way to easily access your money and perform financial transactions outside of bank hours. In order for ABM banking to be most effective, certain security precautions should be taken. Working with a partner, use the space below to create a print advertisement that will help people securely use ABMs. Include at least half of the ABM security tips listed on page 408 of your textbook in your ad.

H. Chapter Notes: Transaction Accounts

Read the fourth section, Transaction Accounts (pages 409–412), in your textbook, and answer the following questions.

1. Briefly describe the three types of accounts offered by financial institutions.

Account Type	Description
Straight transaction account	
Combination account	
Current account	

2. Why is it important to prepare a reconciliation each month?

_____

_____

_____

3. Outline the steps involved in reconciliation.

Step 1: _____

_____

Step 2: _____

_____

Step 3: _____

_____

Step 4: _____

_____

Step 5: _____

_____

I. Activity: Bank Transactions

Bank transactions include cheques, payments, deposits, or withdrawals. Below is a list of transactions for Hui Fung's account for the month of January. Record each transaction in the transaction register below. Insert one number per box. Use the last box in each section to indicate cents. After each transaction, update the balance.

January 1   Opening balance: $65.00

January 4   Deposit: $128.00

January 4   Phone bill, automatic withdrawal: $72.44

January 6   Debit withdrawal, Corner Store: $12.32

January 11   Deposit: $44.00

January 12   Cheque #21, Dr. Lefebvre: $90.45

January 15   Automatic deposit, tax refund: $75.80

January 21   Cash withdrawal: $50.00

January 22   Cheque #22, Molly World: $40.00

January 29   Deposit: $125.45

January 31   Service charge: $3.55

Date	Description	Withdrawal			Deposit			Balance		

Read the fifth section, Writing Cheques (pages 412–417), in your textbook, and use the following organizer to help guide your note-taking. Then answer the questions that follow.

1. Briefly describe the six cheque essentials.

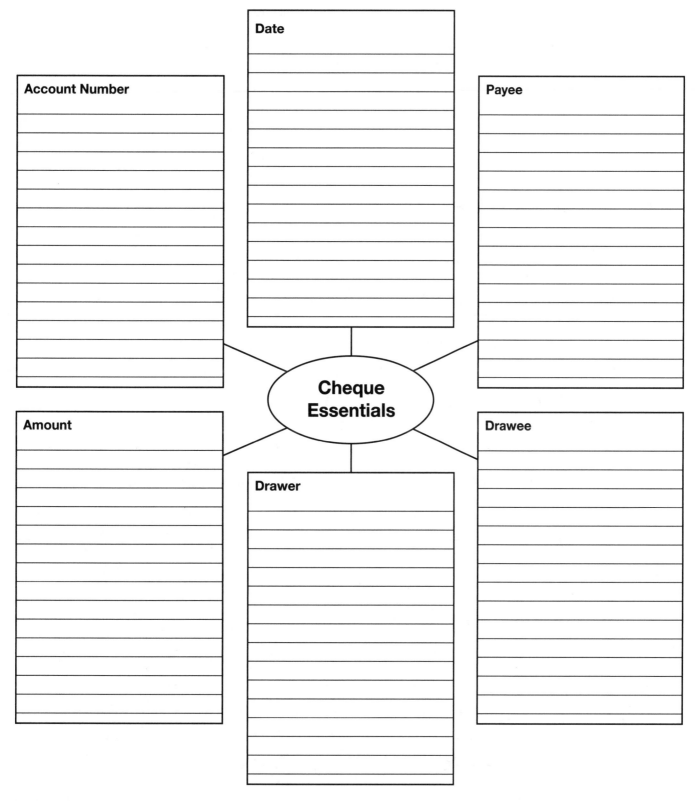

2. What security features exist on cheques?

_____

_____

_____

_____

3. Why would you need to stop payment on a cheque? What details must you provide for the payment to be stopped?

_____

_____

_____

_____

4. Explain the process of cheque clearing.

_____

_____

_____

_____

_____

_____

_____

_____

5. What is magnetic ink character recognition (MICR)? What is it used for?

_____

_____

_____

_____

6. What does it mean to have a hold on a cheque? Why would a bank put a hold on a cheque?

_____

_____

_____

_____

K. Activity: Cheque Elements

1. Study the cheque shown below and answer the following questions to test your knowledge of the essentials of a cheque.

```
                                                              015
NAME   JENNIFER SINGH

ADDRESS   1 SOMETHING STREET                 DATE  July 29, 20___

CITY/TOWN   KINGSTON, ON  K1K 1K1

PAY TO THE    Shelly Norman                          $ 105.73
ORDER OF
          One hundred five                        73/100 DOLLARS

THE BANK
MAIN BRANCH TORONTO
TORONTO, ONTARIO M5X 1S3

MEMO _____          _____ Jennifer Singh _____

  ""015""  ":05552""580":     0127""199""
```

a) Who is the payee? _____

b) Who is the drawer? _____

c) Who is the drawee? _____

d) What is the date of the cheque? _____

e) What is the number of the cheque? _____

f) What is the amount of the cheque? _____

2. Fill out the cheque below using the following information:

Payee: Thomas Roberts   Date: May 16, 20___
Drawer: Gordon Franklin   Amount: $67.80

```
                                                              072
NAME   GORDON FRANKLIN

ADDRESS   1 SOMEWHERE ROAD                   DATE _____

CITY/TOWN   KINGSTON, ON  K1K 1K1

PAY TO THE  _____    $ _____
ORDER OF
          _____        /100 DOLLARS

THE BANK
MAIN BRANCH TORONTO
TORONTO, ONTARIO M5X 1S3

MEMO _____          _____

  ""072""  ":05552""580":     0127""199""
```

L. Chapter Notes: Shared ABM Networks

Read the sixth section, Shared ABM Networks (pages 417–421), in your textbook, and answer the following questions.

1. What is the electronic funds transfer system (EFTS)? What are its benefits to customers and financial institutions? Name three main shared ABM networks.

   _____

   _____

   _____

   _____

   _____

2. Briefly describe Interac Direct Payment, telephone banking, and online banking in the following chart.

Interac Direct Payment	
Telephone banking	
Online banking	

3. How do virtual banks work? Provide three examples of online banks.

   _____

   _____

   _____

   _____

   _____

M. Activity: Transaction Volumes

The table below shows the volume of transactions of the major banks from 2000 to 2005.

Number of Transactions (in millions)							
Delivery Channels	**2000**	**2001**	**2002**	**2003**	**2004**	**2005**	**% Change 2005–2004**
ABM	**1239.4**	**1209.0**	**1206.6**	**1120.8**	**1110.1**	**1056.4**	**–4.8%**
Deposits	244.5	249.9	249.2	256.4	254.6	258.8	1.6%
Withdrawals	875.1	846.2	848.6	761.9	744.1	691.8	–7.0%
Transfers	48.5	45.4	43.7	46.6	53.3	46.7	–12.4%
Bill payments	71.3	67.5	65.1	56.0	58.1	59.0	1.6%
Debit Cards	**1289.8**	**1590.6**	**1749.6**	**1852.7**	**1997.0**	**2125.4**	**6.4%**
PC/Internet Banking	**47.2**	**100.9**	**147.1**	**189.9**	**238.1**	**297.1**	**24.8%**
Transfers	10.5	29.0	43.3	56.6	78.2	101.8	30.2%
Bill payments	36.7	71.9	103.8	133.3	159.9	195.4	22.2%
Telephone Banking	**74.0**	**94.6**	**92.1**	**87.0**	**89.1**	**83.1**	**–6.7%**
Transfers	16.1	17.0	17.3	18.6	19.9	20.3	2.0%
Bill payments	57.9	77.6	74.8	68.4	69.2	62.8	–9.2%

1. Which delivery channel experienced the most growth between 2004 and 2005?

_____

2. In 2005, which delivery channel had the most overall transactions? Which had the least?

_____

3. The number of PC/Internet transactions has grown by 50 million on average since the year 2000. What can this be attributed to?

_____

_____

_____

4. Do you think online banking will ever eliminate the need for branches or ABMs? Explain.

_____

_____

_____

N. Chapter Notes: Other Financial Services

Read the seventh section, Other Financial Services (pages 421–426), in your textbook, and use the following organizer to describe the services offered by financial institutions.

Service	Description
Loans	
Lines of credit	
Credit cards	
Direct deposits	
Money orders and drafts	
Night depositories	
Overdraft protection	
Preauthorized bill payments	
Safety deposit boxes	
Combination service packages	

O. Activity: Interest Rate Comparisons

Each of Canada's Big Five banks offers different rates on borrowing. Visit the websites of three of these banks (RBC Royal Bank, BMO Bank of Montreal, CIBC, TD Canada Trust, or Scotiabank) and compare their features in each area listed below.

Date Researched:			
	Bank 1:	**Bank 2:**	**Bank 3:**
Mortgage rate (1-year closed)			
Mortgage rate (3-year closed)			
Lowest mortgage rate available and the term of that mortgage			
Credit card offered			
Number of different credit card plans			
Name of credit card with the lowest interest rate on purchases			
Annual fee for the credit card bearing the lowest interest rate on purchases			
Cost of the least expensive combination service package for personal accounts with unlimited debits			

P. Chapter Notes: Shopping for a Financial Institution

Read the eighth section, Shopping for a Financial Institution (pages 426–427), in your textbook, and answer the following questions.

1. When shopping for a financial institution, what should you look for?

   _____

   _____

   _____

   _____

   _____

2. Where can you find information about bank services?

   _____

   _____

   _____

   _____

   _____

3. Explain why it is unlikely that Canada will ever be a cashless society.

   _____

   _____

   _____

   _____

   _____

   _____

   _____

   _____

   _____

   _____

4. What are smart cards?

   _____

   _____

   _____

   _____

   _____

Q. Activity: Selecting an Account

The table below lists some different bank account options offered by banks. For each situation described below, evaluate the person's needs and recommend the bank account that best serves these needs for the least amount of money.

Account Name	Monthly Fee	Number of Transactions Included	Minimum Balance to Waive Monthly Fee	Cost of Additional Transactions
Super Banking	$ 7.95	50	$2000.00	$0.65
Simple Banking	$ 3.95	12	n/a	$0.65
Simple Banking Plus	$ 7.00	25	n/a	$0.65
Unlimited Banking	$10.95	unlimited	$3000.00	$0.65
Student Banking	$ 1.25	12	n/a	$0.65
Senior Banking	$ 0	40	n/a	$0.65

1. Sandy just moved out of her parents' home and has a stable job. As she is no longer a student, she has to select a new account. As a student, Sandy found it hard to stick to the 12 transactions covered in her plan, performing about 16 transactions per month. Now that she has moved out, she anticipates needing five to ten more transactions each month.

2. Colby uses cash and debit for all of his needs. His monthly transactions range from 40 to 60. He doesn't like bank fees and usually keeps a daily balance of at least $2500.00 in his account.

3. Kamila used to use her chequing account to pay bills for both herself and her business, using the Unlimited plan. She has since transferred all of her business activities to a separate account and performs only a few transactions each month in her personal account.

R. Case Study: Technology and Banking: A Survey of Canadian Attitudes (2004)

Banking used to be a 10:00 A.M. to 3:00 P.M. Monday-to-Friday service that could be conducted only at one's home bank branch. Times have changed. Canadians are now banking 24/7 from almost any location imaginable, using a wide range of access options, from in person at a branch, to online while in another country, to using a cellphone from the dock at the cottage. In fact, Canadians are world leaders in the use of both debit cards and ABMs.

Canadians feel strongly that technology has made their personal banking more convenient, with 50 percent reporting that it has made it much more convenient. There are three main reasons why Canadian consumers like the convenience of banking technologies: they can conduct their banking anywhere (50 percent); they are not dependent on bank hours (43 percent); it saves them time and running around to conduct banking transactions (26 percent). Not only is the ability to choose where and when to bank important to consumers, but a range of options in how to bank is also a top priority. Technology has improved banking for customers through the availability of a national network of ABMs (88 percent), the ability to use debit cards as a means of payment (88 percent), and the ability to conduct transactions by telephone or online (77 percent).

Although Canadians are using a variety of methods to access banking services, online banking has shown the most significant year-over-year growth. Between 2002 and 2004, online banking continued to gain in popularity, with 42 percent of Canadians reporting that they banked online, an increase of 8 percent over 2002. When asked to name the primary way in which they conduct the majority of their financial transactions, 23 percent reported that it was online, a figure that had tripled since 2000.

In the 2004 survey, individuals were asked about the main way in which they pay most of their regular bills. Online bill payment emerged as the number one option, with over one-quarter of Canadians using it as their preferred method. In fact, almost two-thirds (64 percent) of all bills were paid through electronic methods. This is consistent with Canadian Payments Association (CPA) data showing that 75 percent of items flowing through the clearing settlement system (ACSS) were electronic items versus 25 percent paper-based. Ten years earlier, it was the reverse, with 30 percent being electronic items and 70 percent paper-based.

1. What are the three main reasons Canadians like banking technologies?

   _____

   _____

2. What factors do you believe have influenced the growth of online banking, including electronic bill payment? What factors may be preventing people from trying online banking?

   _____

   _____

   _____

   _____

Business Word Bank		
automated banking machines	drawer	reconciliation
bank rate	line of credit	service charge
caisses populaires	money order	signature card
cancelled cheques	money supply	staledated cheque
chartered bank	online banks	stop payment
cheque clearing	outstanding cheques	straight transaction account
combination account	overdraft	term loan
current account	payee	transaction account
direct deposit	postdating	transaction register
drawee	preauthorized debit	

Use the terms given in the word bank to complete the following statements:

1. A(n) _____ is entitled to call itself a "bank" because it operates under the *Bank Act*.

2. The _____ is all of the money in circulation.

3. The _____ is the minimum rate of interest the Bank of Canada charges for loans made to chartered banks.

4. _____ and credit unions are co-operatives that perform banking functions for people who are members.

5. When opening a bank account, the bank keeps a copy of the way a customer writes his or her name on a(n) _____.

6. _____ allow customers to use a computer terminal to deposit funds, make withdrawals, and do other banking transactions.

7. A(n) _____ is used by customers to pay for goods and services and other needs. Transactions are recorded on a(n) _____.

8. A(n) _____ is a basic account to pay personal and household bills. A(n) _____ offers both savings and chequing features.

9. A processing fee or _____ is levied on each cheque unless covered by a service plan.

10. A cheque that has been cashed and paid by the financial institution is a(n) _____.

11. Businesses use a(n) _____ for their banking needs.

12. Every month, you should prepare a(n) _____ to bring your records and the bank's records into agreement.

13. _____ are cheques written but not yet cashed.

14. A cheque more than six months past its written date is a(n) _____. Putting a future date on a cheque is known as _____.

15. Cheques carry several names: the _____ is the person or business to whom the cheque is written; the _____ is the financial institution; the _____ is the person who signed the cheque and from whose account the money will be taken.

16. A(n) _____ is an order requesting a financial institution to not pay a particular cheque.

17. The processing of cheques and the settling of account balances among financial institutions is known as _____.

18. _____, or virtual banks, do not have actual branches but are accessed via the Internet, ABMs, telephone, and independent professionals.

19. A(n) _____ involves borrowing money and paying it back at a specified time, while a(n) _____ is a one-time-approval loan that gives the borrower access to credit up to a maximum agreed-upon amount.

20. A(n) _____ is a transfer of funds directly into an account.

21. A(n) _____ or draft is a form of guaranteed payment.

22. Having a(n) _____ means that you wrote a cheque for more money than you have in your account.

23. A(n) _____ allows the authorization of regular and automatic withdrawals from your bank account.

CHAPTER 14: SAVINGS AND INVESTING

A. Business Vocabulary

In Chapter 14, you'll encounter some terms related to savings and investing. Before you begin working with the chapter, browse through the pages and look for the bolded key terms. Use the left-hand side of the chart below to write any words you don't immediately understand. Then, when you arrive at the section featuring the word, write its definition in the middle column. Use the last column to note any relevant examples.

Term	Textbook Definition	Examples

B. Chapter Notes: Savings and Investing

Read the first section, Savings and Investing (pages 435–437), in your textbook, and answer the following questions.

1. What are the benefits and drawbacks of savings deposited in a financial institution?

   _____

   _____

   _____

   _____

2. What is investing? List its advantages and disadvantages compared to saving.

   _____

   _____

   _____

   _____

   _____

3. Explain three reasons why people save.

Need for Saving	Description
Emergency needs	
Short- and long-term goals	
Security and future needs	

C. Activity: Saving for Home Repairs

One of the biggest expenses a person will encounter will be the purchase and maintenance of a home. Everyone who owns a home should set up a savings plan to prepare for future home repairs.

1. The chart below illustrates the projected life expectancy of various components of a home and the expected cost to replace them. Calculate the amount that needs to be saved each month to ensure that the cost of replacement can be met. Assume that no interest is accrued on the savings. The first calculation has been done for you.

	Life Expectancy (in years)	Expected Replacement Cost	Monthly Savings Required
Roof shingles	10	$ 2 174.00	10 × 12 months = 120 months; $2 174.00 ÷ 120 = $18.12/month
Refrigerator	6	$ 750.00	
Oven	6	$ 900.00	
Washer	8	$ 525.00	
Dryer	8	$ 475.00	
Exterior painting	6	$ 3 750.00	
Windows	15	$12 000.00	
Doors	15	$ 5 500.00	
Driveway	9	$ 4 200.00	

2. What is the total amount that should be saved each month?

_____

_____

3. Assume that when you moved in, the fridge was four years old. How would you adjust your monthly savings, assuming the replacement cost is the same?

_____

_____

_____

D. Chapter Notes: Selecting a Savings Plan

Read the second section, Selecting a Savings Plan (pages 438–440), in your textbook, and answer the following questions.

1. What happens to the purchasing power of money without a savings plan?

   _____

   _____

2. Explain why a bank pays interest on a deposit.

   _____

   _____

   _____

3. What is a rate of return?

   _____

   _____

4. Explain the difference between simple interest and compound interest.

   _____

   _____

   _____

   _____

   _____

   _____

5. How much of your money is insured when deposited in a bank? What is the name of the agency that governs this protection?

   _____

   _____

   _____

   _____

6. Why is it important for investors to keep some liquid investments? Provide some examples of liquid and non-liquid investments.

   _____

   _____

   _____

   _____

E. Activity: Simple vs. Compound Interest

Simple interest is interest calculated on the principal, or the amount deposited. Compound interest is interest calculated on the principal plus any interest already earned. Compounding makes your savings grow faster than simple interest. To see how compounding can make your savings grow, let's compare it to simple interest.

1. How much interest would you earn on an $8 000.00 deposit with an annual interest rate of 5 percent with simple interest over six years? The first calculation has been done for you.

	Beginning of the Year	During the Year	End of the Year
Year 1	$ 8 000.00	+(5% of $8 000.00 = $400.00)	$ 8 400.00
Year 2	$ 8 400.00		
Year 3			
Year 4			
Year 5			
Year 6			

2. If the same $8 000.00 is compounded annually for six years at 5 percent interest, how much would you earn?

	Beginning of the Year	During the Year	End of the Year
Year 1	$ 8 000.00	+(5% of $8 000.00 = $400.00)	$ 8 400.00
Year 2	$ 8 400.00		
Year 3			
Year 4			
Year 5			
Year 6			

3. For each year, calculate the difference between simple and compound interest.

Year 1	
Year 2	
Year 3	
Year 4	
Year 5	
Year 6	

F. Activity: The Pepsi Puzzle

Did you know that, by buying a Pepsi from the vending machine each day, you could be drinking away a fortune without giving it much thought? Consider the following, assuming that one 355 mL can of Pepsi is $1.25.

1. Calculate the annual cost of your Pepsi for one academic year (189 days), assuming that you purchase one can each day.

    _____

2. Assuming that the price stayed the same during your entire high school career, how much would you spend on Pepsi over four years?

    _____

3. Now imagine that you have graduated high school and instead have taken your annual Pepsi spending and invested it at an interest rate of 8 percent, compounded annually. Calculate its value 10 years, 20 years, 30 years, and 40 years after graduation.

    The formula for compound interest is $FV = PV(1 + i)^n$, where
    * FV is the future value you are attempting to calculate
    * PV is the present value of money you have to start
    * i is the interest rate expressed as a decimal
    * n is the number of compounding periods

    For example, $1000.00 invested at 8 percent for nine years is
    $FV = 1000.00(1 + 0.08)^9$
    $FV = 1000.00(1.99)$
    $FV = \$1999.00$

    a) 10 years after graduation

    _____

    b) 20 years after graduation

    _____

    c) 30 years after graduation

    _____

    d) 40 years after graduation

    _____

G. Chapter Notes: Common Savings Plans

Read the third section, Common Savings Plans (pages 441–447), in your textbook, and answer the following questions.

1. What are three benefits of a savings plan?

_____

_____

2. What is a savings account? How does the interest paid compare to other savings plans?

_____

_____

3. What is the difference between term deposits and guaranteed investment certificates (GICs)?

_____

_____

_____

_____

_____

4. What is a registered retirement savings plan (RRSP)?

_____

_____

_____

_____

_____

5. Why is it unwise to withdraw money from an RRSP before retirement?

_____

_____

_____

_____

_____

6. What is a registered education savings plan (RESP)?

_____

_____

_____

_____

_____

H. Activity: The Power of Compounding Interest

The *Who Wants to Become a Millionaire?* chart on page 443 of your textbook illustrates the power of compounding and investing early for your retirement. Were you surprised that, although Anthony had invested more, Sarah had more money in her RRSP at age 65? The chart below illustrates how their money grew each year.

NOTES:

- Sarah's initial contribution is made at the beginning of age 19.
- Anthony's initial contribution is made at the beginning of age 27.
- Anthony's final contribution occurs at the beginning of age 65 with one year of compounding left.
- The final value is the value at the end of age 65.
- Interest is compounded annually at a rate of 10 percent.

Age	Sarah's RRSP	Yearly Contribution	Yearly Interest	Anthony's RRSP	Yearly Contribution	Yearly Interest
19	$ 2 000.00	$ 2 000.00				
20	$ 4 200.00	$ 2 000.00	$ 200.00			
21	$ 6 620.00	$ 2 000.00	$ 420.00			
22	$ 9 282.00	$ 2 000.00	$ 662.00			
23	$ 12 210.20	$ 2 000.00	$ 928.20			
24	$ 15 431.22	$ 2 000.00	$ 1 221.02			
25	$ 18 974.34	$ 2 000.00	$ 1 543.12			
26	$ 22 871.78	$ 2 000.00	$ 1 897.43			
27	$ 25 158.95		$ 2 287.18	$ 2 000.00	$ 2 000.00	
28	$ 27 674.85		$ 2 515.90	$ 4 200.00	$ 2 000.00	$ 200.00
29	$ 30 442.33		$ 2 767.48	$ 6 620.00	$ 2 000.00	$ 420.00
30	$ 33 486.57		$ 3 044.23	$ 9 282.00	$ 2 000.00	$ 662.00
31	$ 36 835.22		$ 3 348.66	$ 12 210.20	$ 2 000.00	$ 928.20
32	$ 40 518.75		$ 3 683.52	$ 15 431.22	$ 2 000.00	$ 1 221.02
33	$ 44 570.62		$ 4 051.87	$ 18 974.34	$ 2 000.00	$ 1 543.12
34	$ 49 027.68		$ 4 457.06	$ 22 871.78	$ 2 000.00	$ 1 897.43
35	$ 53 930.45		$ 4 902.77	$ 27 158.95	$ 2 000.00	$ 2 287.18
36	$ 59 323.50		$ 5 393.05	$ 31 874.85	$ 2 000.00	$ 2 715.90
37	$ 65 255.85		$ 5 932.35	$ 37 062.33	$ 2 000.00	$ 3 187.48
38	$ 71 781.43		$ 6 525.58	$ 42 768.57	$ 2 000.00	$ 3 706.23
39	$ 78 959.57		$ 7 178.14	$ 49 045.42	$ 2 000.00	$ 4 276.86

Age	Sarah's RRSP	Yearly Contribution	Yearly Interest	Anthony's RRSP	Yearly Contribution	Yearly Interest
40	$ 86 855.53		$ 7 895.96	$ 55 949.97	$ 2 000.00	$ 4 904.54
41	$ 95 541.09		$ 8 685.55	$ 63 544.96	$ 2 000.00	$ 5 595.00
42	$ 105 095.19		$ 9 554.11	$ 71 899.46	$ 2 000.00	$ 6 354.50
43	$ 115 604.71		$ 10 509.52	$ 81 089.41	$ 2 000.00	$ 7 189.95
44	$ 127 165.18		$ 11 560.47	$ 91 198.35	$ 2 000.00	$ 8 108.94
45	$ 139 881.70		$ 12 716.52	$102 318.18	$ 2 000.00	$ 9 119.83
46	$ 153 869.87		$ 13 988.17	$114 550.00	$ 2 000.00	$ 10 231.82
47	$ 169 256.86		$ 15 386.99	$128 005.00	$ 2 000.00	$ 11 455.00
48	$ 186 182.55		$ 16 925.69	$142 805.50	$ 2 000.00	$ 12 800.50
49	$ 204 800.80		$ 18 618.25	$159 086.05	$ 2 000.00	$ 14 280.55
50	$ 225 280.88		$ 20 480.08	$176 994.65	$ 2 000.00	$ 15 908.60
51	$ 247 808.97		$ 22 528.09	$196 694.12	$ 2 000.00	$ 17 699.47
52	$ 272 589.87		$ 24 780.90	$218 363.53	$ 2 000.00	$ 19 669.41
53	$ 299 848.85		$ 27 258.99	$242 199.88	$ 2 000.00	$ 21 836.35
54	$ 329 833.74		$ 29 984.89	$268 419.87	$ 2 000.00	$ 24 219.99
55	$ 362 817.11		$ 32 983.37	$297 261.86	$ 2 000.00	$ 26 841.99
56	$ 399 098.82		$ 36 281.71	$328 988.05	$ 2 000.00	$ 29 726.19
57	$ 439 008.71		$ 39 909.88	$363 886.85	$ 2 000.00	$ 32 898.80
58	$ 482 909.58		$ 43 900.87	$402 275.53	$ 2 000.00	$ 36 388.68
59	$ 531 200.53		$ 48 290.96	$444 503.09	$ 2 000.00	$ 40 227.55
60	$ 584 320.59		$ 53 120.05	$490 953.40	$ 2 000.00	$ 44 450.31
61	$ 642 752.65		$ 58 432.06	$542 048.74	$ 2 000.00	$ 49 095.34
62	$ 707 027.91		$ 64 275.26	$598 253.61	$ 2 000.00	$ 54 204.87
63	$ 777 730.70		$ 70 702.79	$660 078.97	$ 2 000.00	$ 59 825.36
64	$ 855 503.77		$ 77 773.07	$728 086.87	$ 2 000.00	$ 66 007.90
65	$ 941 054.15		$ 85 550.38	$802 895.56	$ 2 000.00	$ 72 808.69
Final Value	$1 035 159.56		$ 94 105.41	$883 185.11		$ 80 289.56
Total Contribution		$16 000.00			$78 000.00	
Total Interest			$1 019 159.56			$805 185.11

1. At the end of age 65, what was the difference in the total RRSP amount between Anthony and Sarah?

_____

_____

_____

_____

_____

_____

2. Sarah made only eight contributions, totalling $16 000.00, while Anthony made 39 contributions, totalling $78 000.00. At the age of 65, what was the difference in the total interest earned by Sarah and the total interest earned by Anthony?

_____

_____

_____

_____

_____

_____

3. If Anthony's and Sarah's savings had been calculated using simple interest, who do you think would have earned more interest by the age of 65? Explain why.

_____

_____

_____

_____

_____

4. If you wanted to contribute $2000.00 per year like Anthony and Sarah, you would have to save $5.48 per day. How would you encourage your peers to start this savings plan?

_____

_____

_____

_____

_____

I. Chapter Notes: Common Forms of Investment

Read the fourth section, Common Forms of Investment (pages 447–456), in your textbook, and answer the following questions.

1. What are the differences between risky and safe investments? What do investors usually look for when investing?

2. Why do good investors diversify their investments?

3. What are Canada Savings Bonds? What are the advantages of purchasing Canada Savings Bonds?

4. What is a bond? Why would a business offer bonds?

5. How do bondholders make money on bonds? What happens if they want to sell their bonds before they mature?

6. What is the difference between a bull market and a bear market?

_____

_____

7. What factors influence stock prices?

_____

_____

_____

_____

8. Compare the advantages and disadvantages of common stock and preferred stock.

Type of Stock	Advantages	Disadvantages
Common stock		
Preferred stock		

9. List three ways the Toronto Stock Exchange (TSX) makes a profit.

_____

_____

_____

10. Explain the negotiation process of buying and selling stocks.

_____

_____

_____

11. List two advantages and two disadvantages of online investing.

_____

_____

_____

_____

_____

12. What are two components of a stock quotation? What do newspaper stock quotations usually list?

_____

_____

_____

_____

_____

_____

_____

_____

13. What are mutual funds? What are the benefits of investing in a mutual fund?

_____

_____

_____

_____

_____

_____

_____

_____

14. Why would someone consider real estate as an investment?

_____

_____

_____

_____

15. How might an old baseball card be an investment?

_____

_____

_____

_____

J. Activity: Investments

Imagine that you have inherited $25 000 and have decided to make various investments to increase the value of your inheritance. Each investment is made at the beginning of the year and is liquidated or sold at the end of the year.

January 1

Purchased shares of stock for $7000

Purchased a $2000 GIC, paying 6 percent annually

Invested $5000 in mutual funds

Purchased a rare baseball card for $4400

Bought an interest in a time-share condominium for $5800

Deposited the remaining $800 in a savings account

December 31

Received $600 in dividends during the year and sold the stock for $7990

GIC matured and was worth $2120 when redeemed

Liquidated mutual funds for $5900

Sold baseball card for $5100

Sold interest in condominium for $5100

$832 was in savings account when closed

1. How much money was earned on each investment during the year? Show your calculations.

   Stock: _____

   GIC: _____

   Mutual funds: _____

   Baseball card: _____

   Condominium: _____

   Savings account: _____

2. What was the rate of return on each of these investments? Show your calculations.

   Stock: _____

   GIC: _____

   Mutual funds: _____

   Baseball card: _____

   Condominium: _____

   Savings account: _____

3. Which investment seemed to be the best one? Why?

   _____

4. Which investment seemed to be the worst one? Why?

   _____

K. Chapter Notes: Business Investments

Read the fifth section, Business Investments (pages 456–458), in your textbook, and use the following organizer to guide your note-taking.

Explain why businesses invest.

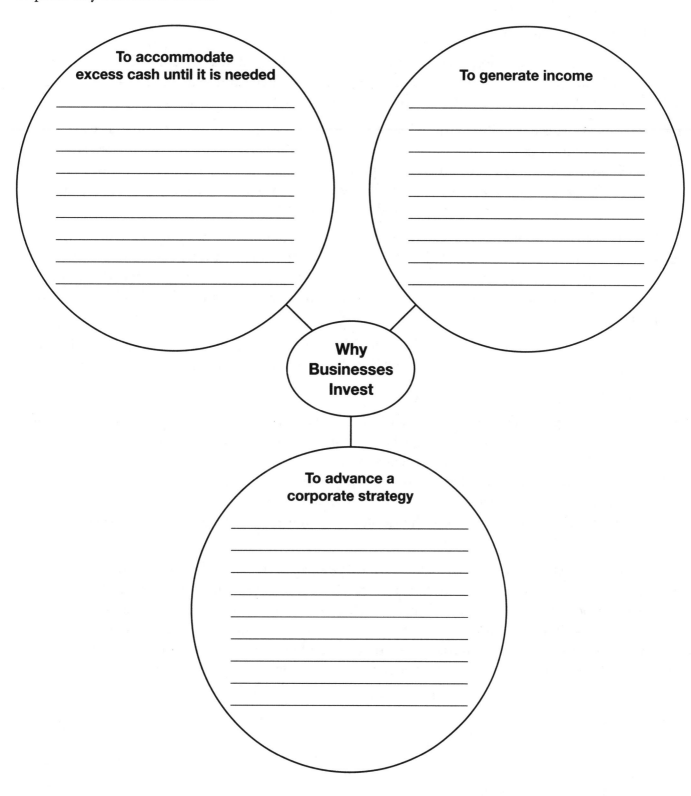

L. Case Study: Contemplating Collectibles

If you have much space for storage, your attic and garage might be stuffed with old furniture, books, and other items you've held onto over the years. If this is the case, you may be sitting on a few valuable collectibles just waiting to make you money. That said, you are just as likely to be looking at little more than a pile of junk.

All Things Old Made New Again

140 000 000 BCE: A young Allosaurus missteps and finds itself mired in a sinkhole hidden beneath the underbrush. Millions of years later, an amateur paleontologist helps him out—or at least what was left of his head. In 2005, the Allosaurus's restored skull sells for the high price of $600.

1908: Honus Wagner of the Pittsburgh Pirates hits his tenth home run and ends the year with a .354 batting average, marking one of the best years of his career. The next year, the American Tobacco Company commemorates Wagner by putting a trading card inside its cigarette packages. Fewer than 60 make it into stores before it is discovered that Honus is vehemently against smoking. In 2000, Wagner's cigarette trading card is sold on eBay for $1.1 million.

1962: Stan Lee creates a superhero who has to worry about rent, his ailing aunt, and passing his next test—all in addition to saving the world. Peter Parker's misadventure with a radioactive spider hits the stands with a $0.12 cover price. And, in 2006, the first edition of The Amazing Spider-Man is among the most valuable comics, with a price around $6000 or more, according to Wizard: The Guide To Comics pricing guide.

These are all examples of the strange and wonderful world of collectibles. While there is no denying the thrill of owning a juvenile Allosaurus skull, is collecting really a form of investment?

All That Glitters ...

The reason we began by discussing a fossil, a comic, and a baseball card is that people have no qualms about calling them collectibles. However, when you speak about diamonds, gold, and other precious materials, people tend to call them investments. In theory, these materials could be termed collectibles because their price is based more on what people are willing to pay for them (or market value) than on their actual intrinsic value. But in the practical world, precious metals have an intrinsic value. This value is based on rarity and the fact that, if you melt it, burn it, or bend it, you still have the same atomic substance in the end.

What makes collectibles different is that even a little damage can erase all of a collectible's value. This is because a collectible's value is based on emotional factors like nostalgia. These emotional factors can be as erratic as they are powerful. If you were asked whether people would be willing to pay more for a dinosaur skull or a baseball card, even if you chose one over the other you would give them both a higher value than, say, a torn up baseball card or a box of bone fragments. Those items you would probably call worthless (unless you are an archaeologist or a fan of papier-mâché).

1. Why can diamonds and gold be considered collectibles?

   _____

   _____

   _____

   _____

   _____

   _____

   _____

   _____

   _____

2. What gives metals value that other collectibles don't possess?

   _____

   _____

   _____

   _____

   _____

   _____

   _____

   _____

   _____

3. Based on this case study, do you believe that collectibles are a good investment? Why or why not?

   _____

   _____

   _____

   _____

   _____

   _____

   _____

   _____

   _____

M. Review

Business Word Bank		
ask price	face value	rate of return
bear market	growth companies	real estate
bid price	GICs	RESP
blue chip companies	interest	RRSP
bonds	investing	savings
bull market	market value	savings plan
Canada Savings Bonds	maturity date	securities
collectibles	mutual fund	simple interest
common stock	online investing	term deposits
compound interest	preferred stock	treasury bills
diversify	principal	

Use the terms given in the word bank to complete the following statements:

1. Consumers can put extra money into _____ and save it for future use, or use the money to earn extra income through _____.

2. A(n) _____ is a regular method of putting money aside in order to reach a financial goal.

3. The _____, or yield, is the expression of _____ earned as a percentage.

4. Interest calculated on the amount deposited, or the _____, is _____. Interest calculated on the principal plus any interest already earned is called _____.

5. _____ and _____ are savings plans where a fixed sum of money is deposited for a specific length of time at a fixed rate of interest.

6. Individuals may save money in a(n) _____ to minimize income tax now and provide income in retirement.

7. Students can benefit from a(n) _____, which is a tax-sheltered plan designed to help pay for post-secondary education.

8. Knowledgeable investors _____ their investments by spreading their money across a number of different investments.

9. Investing in _____ involves making a loan to the Government of Canada. On the _____, the investor is paid the _____ plus interest.

10. To raise money, corporations sell _____, including stocks and _____, which are guaranteed to be repaid with interest at a specified future date. If necessary, investors can sell these at _____, or the price another investor is willing to pay.

11. In a(n) _____ the demand for and prices of stocks is generally high; when the supply of stocks exceeds the demand there is a(n) _____.

12. Investors can purchase _____, and have the right to vote on company business, or _____, which gives them dividends at a fixed rate.

13. _____ are large, well-established companies that make regular dividend payments. _____ reinvest profits into their operations instead of paying shareholder dividends.

14. _____ involves buying and selling stocks on the Internet.

15. Stock quotations include a(n) _____, which is the highest price anyone is willing to pay for a particular stock, and a(n) _____, which is the lowest selling price that another investor is willing to accept for that stock.

16. A(n) _____ is a pool of money from many investors that is set up and managed by a professional investment management company to buy and sell securities of other corporations.

17. Some people invest in _____ by purchasing a house or other piece of property; others believe their _____ will increase in value over time.

18. A business with excess cash may invest in _____, a form of short-term government bond issued in large denominations.

CHAPTER 15: CREDIT

A. Business Vocabulary

In Chapter 15, you'll encounter some terms related to credit. Before you begin working with the chapter, browse through the pages and look for the bolded key terms. Use the left-hand side of the chart below to write any words you don't immediately understand. Then, when you arrive at the section featuring the word, write its definition in the middle column. Use the last column to note any relevant examples.

Term	Textbook Definition	Examples

B. Chapter Notes: The Wonderful World of Credit

Read the first section, The Wonderful World of Credit (pages 467–472), in your textbook, and answer the following questions.

1. Define credit. Who are creditors and debtors?

   _____

   _____

   _____

   _____

2. Describe the advantages and disadvantages of using consumer credit.

Advantages of Consumer Credit	Disadvantages of Consumer Credit

3. Describe why each of the following uses credit.
   a) Consumers: _____

   _____

   _____

   _____

   b) Governments: _____

   _____

   _____

   _____

   c) Businesses: _____

   _____

   _____

   _____

4. Describe the advantages and disadvantages of business credit.

Advantages of Business Credit	Disadvantages of Business Credit

5. Describe three ways that a business can grant credit.

_____

_____

_____

_____

_____

_____

_____

_____

6. Why might granting credit to other businesses be risky for a supplier?

_____

_____

_____

_____

_____

_____

_____

_____

C. Activity: Viewpoints on Credit

Joshua and Katherine are a newly married couple. Although they have many things in common, one area where they differ is their views on credit. Joshua uses his two credit cards for every purchase where credit is available. He rarely carries cash but pays off his credit card balances in full every month. Katherine, on the other hand, does not like credit. She has no credit cards and pays for all of her purchases with cash or by debit.

1. With a partner, discuss the advantages and disadvantages of Joshua's and Katherine's views on credit. List at least three advantages and three disadvantages for each person's view of credit.

Joshua's View of Credit		Katherine's View of Credit	
Advantages	**Disadvantages**	**Advantages**	**Disadvantages**

2. Given the list of advantages and disadvantages, do you feel that one person's strategy is superior to the other's? Why or why not?

_____

_____

_____

_____

3. Joshua and Katherine demonstrate two extremes of the credit continuum. Where do you think you fall on this continuum? Do you think you're more like Katherine or Joshua? Explain.

_____

_____

_____

_____

D. Chapter Notes: Types and Sources of Credit

Read the second section, Types and Sources of Credit (pages 473–479), in your textbook, and answer the following questions.

1. How are payments determined on bank-issued credit cards? How is interest calculated?

   _____

   _____

   _____

2. List the five advantages of credit cards over other forms of credit.

   1. _____

      _____

   2. _____

      _____

   3. _____

      _____

   4. _____

      _____

   5. _____

      _____

3. For a business, what are the costs associated with accepting credit cards?

   _____

   _____

   _____

   _____

4. Briefly describe travel and entertainment cards.

   _____

   _____

5. Why would a retailer offer its own credit card? What are the drawbacks of doing so?

   _____

   _____

   _____

   _____

6. Explain how installment sales credit works. Who would use this type of credit?

_____

_____

_____

_____

_____

_____

7. Explain why consumers and businesses would want to take out loans.

_____

_____

8. Briefly describe the five types of loans.

Type of Loan	Description
Term loan	
Lease	
Demand loan	
Student loan	
Mortgage loan	

E. Activity: Methods of Payment

There are a number of ways to pay for a purchase. In the chart below, put an x in the appropriate column(s) to indicate whether a family is more likely to pay for the item with cash, a credit card, or an installment plan. More than one answer may be acceptable in certain cases. Give a reason for your decision in each case.

Item	Cash	Credit Card	Installment Plan	Reason
Big screen TV				
Toothpaste				
Notepad				
New car				
Movie				
Motorcycle				
Dining room set				
Toaster				
Computer				
Washer and dryer				

F. Chapter Notes: The Cost of Credit

Read the third section, The Cost of Credit (pages 480–482), in your textbook, and answer the following questions.

1. What are the six factors in determining the interest cost of credit?

_____

_____

_____

_____

2. Why do short-term loans tend to have lower rates?

_____

_____

_____

_____

3. How do you calculate simple interest?

_____

4. What is the formula for the total cost of a loan?

_____

5. What factors must be taken into consideration when calculating interest on a loan?

_____

_____

_____

6. Why would collateral be required as security for a loan?

_____

_____

_____

_____

7. Why is having a good credit rating important?

_____

_____

_____

_____

G. Activity: Credit Notices

1. Find several newspaper or direct mail advertisements for large consumer items such as cars, recreational vehicles, furniture, appliances, etc. Describe or tape in a picture of the item being advertised, including the credit information that was included in the ad. For example, many car dealerships advertise lease rates and conditions in their ads. Pay particular attention to the fine print at the bottom of the ad as credit information is often recorded there.

2. Summarize the credit information in your own words.

_____

_____

_____

_____

_____

H. Activity: Calculating the Cost of Credit

When you purchase goods or services on credit, you have to pay the purchase price of the product or service plus interest or finance charges and possibly some additional fees. The more money you borrow (or the more credit you use), the more you pay in interest or finance charges.

1. Imagine that you have just made a $1200.00 purchase at a major department store. You pay for the item using a store-issued credit card, which charges 30 percent interest on the unpaid balance. Interest is calculated monthly and added to your account at the end of each month. You agree to make monthly payments of $200.00, including interest, and you make no additional purchases until your account is fully paid. Complete the following chart. The first calculation has been done for you.

Month	Beginning Balance	Monthly Payment	Monthly Interest Payment	Amount Paid on Balance	Ending Balance
March	$1200.00	$200.00	$30.00	$170.00	$1030.00
April	$1030.00				
May					
June					
July					
August					
September					

2. How long did it take you to pay your account in full?

_____

3. How much did your $1200.00 purchase cost using credit?

_____

4. What was the total finance charge on your purchase?

_____

I. Chapter Notes: Credit Worthiness

Read the fourth section, Credit Worthiness (pages 483–489), in your textbook, and answer the following questions.

1. What is credit worthiness?

   _____

   _____

   _____

   _____

2. When applying for a loan, a lender evaluates a borrower's credit worthiness by examining an individual's or business's character, capacity, and capital—the three Cs of credit. Briefly describe how and why each of these is assessed. Identify the one question a lender seeks to answer for each characteristic.

Character	Capacity	Capital

3. What is a credit bureau? Who are its main customers?

   _____

   _____

   _____

   _____

   _____

4. What is a credit rating?

_____

_____

_____

_____

5. List the actions that can influence whether a borrower's credit rating is good or poor.

A good credit rating results when a borrower...	A lower credit rating results when a borrower...

6. Why would a student need someone to co-sign a loan?

_____

_____

_____

_____

7. What are four signs of credit crisis?

_____

_____

_____

_____

8. List six ways to deal with a credit crisis.

1. _____

2. _____

3. _____

4. _____

5. _____

6. _____

J. Activity: The Three Cs of Credit

1. Imagine that you are a loans officer, reviewing a customer's loan application. Listed below are some questions you might ask to help evaluate the applicant's credit worthiness, or ability to assume and pay back the debt. Indicate which of the three Cs of credit (character, capacity, and capital) each question attempts to assess by placing an x in the appropriate column.

Information Requested	Character	Capacity	Capital
What are the balances in your bank accounts?			
Do you pay bills on time?			
Do you have a permanent job?			
Where do you work and how long have you been at your present job?			
Do you own or rent your current house/apartment?			
Do you have any dependents?			
How much money do you currently owe?			
What are your current expenses?			
What is the value of your assets?			

2. Explain how you would use your assessment of the applicant's three Cs to make a decision about whether or not to approve the loan. Which C do you think is most important? Why?

_____

_____

_____

_____

_____

_____

_____

_____

_____

_____

K. Case Study: Payday Loans

For people who can't get a credit card, or those who have a poor credit history that limits access to other forms of credit, payday loans are the lenders of last resort (loan sharks excepted). They are also the most expensive.

The concept is simple enough. You don't have enough money to make it to your next paycheque. So you go to a payday lender who will lend you, say, $100 for two weeks until your next paycheque. Of course, they levy fees, service charges, and interest on that loan that will add $20 to the cost of that $100 loan. You get your $100 instantly and write out a cheque for $120 dated on the day of your next paycheque. That works out to an annual interest rate of over 500 percent.

But that's not the worst of it. One lawyer represented a woman who borrowed $520. She kept rolling over her loan every two weeks for more than two years because she was never able to repay the original loan. Each rollover cost her $130 in fees and interest. By the time she was able to come up with the full amount owing (some 30 months later), she had paid more than $8000 in fees and interest.

The payday loan companies defend their business, saying they provide a much-needed service. They point out (correctly) that banks aren't interested in lending a few hundred dollars for a week or two.

Several class-action suits have been filed against providers of payday loans. And governments are looking into regulating the industry.

In the meantime, Ottawa bankruptcy lawyer Stanley Kershman, the author of *Put Your Debt on a Diet*, has some advice for anyone thinking of taking out a payday loan. "Don't," he writes. "If money is short between paydays … find another way of surviving your budget shortfall."

1. What is a payday loan? Why do consumers seek them out?

   _____

   _____

   _____

   _____

2. What fees are levied by payday loan companies? How do these compare to bank fees?

   _____

   _____

   _____

   _____

3. List some alternatives to payday loans for covering a shortfall between paycheques.

   _____

   _____

   _____

   _____

L. Review

Business Word Bank		
capacity	credit	demand loan
capital	credit rating	installment sales credit
character	credit worthiness	lease
collateral	creditor	term loan
consolidation loan	debtor	three Cs of credit

Use the terms given in the word bank to complete the following statements:

1. _____ is the privilege of using someone else's money for a period of time.

2. A(n) _____ is a person or business that buys on credit or obtains a loan; a(n) _____ is the person or business that grants a loan or sells on credit.

3. _____ is a credit plan that requires a purchaser to make a down payment and then fixed regular payments.

4. A(n) _____ is a form of installment credit in which the borrower makes regular fixed payments over a set period of time.

5. A(n) _____ allows you to rent something for a period of time at a set cost.

6. A(n) _____ is a short-term loan with flexible terms of repayment. This type of loan often requires _____, something of value that can be taken and sold if the loan is not repaid on time.

7. A person's ability to assume and pay back credit is known as _____.

8. The _____ are used to determine credit worthiness. They include a borrower's willingness to repay a loan when it is due, known as _____; the ability to make the payments on a debt, which is the borrower's _____; and _____, which is the value of the borrower's assets.

9. A borrower's _____ is an indication of the level of risk that the consumer, business, or government will pose if credit is granted.

10. A borrower who is having trouble paying multiple debts may obtain a(n) _____ to combine several loans into one.

Credits

Chapter 2

30 Adapted from Industry Canada, "E-commerce in Service Industries - 2003," http://strategis.ic.gc.ca/epic/site/ecom-come.nsf/en/qy00016e.html. Reproduced with the permission of the Minister of Public Works and Government Services. 2007.

Chapter 3

46 "Business Ethics Case Studies: Whistleblowing & the Environment: The Case of Avco Environmental" by Chris MacDonald (Business Ethics). 2005. http://www.businessethics.ca/cases/wb-env1.html. Used with permission.

Chapter 4

54 Adapted from *The World of Business: A Canadian Profile*, Student Workbook 4th Ed. by Murphy/Wilson/Notman. 2002. Reprinted with permission of Nelson, a division of Thomson Learning: www.thomsonrights.com. Fax: 1-800-730-2215;
55 Adapted from *The World of Business: A Canadian Profile*, Student Workbook 4th Ed. by Murphy/Wilson/Notman. 2002. Reprinted with permission of Nelson, a division of Thomson Learning: www.thomsonrights.com. Fax: 1-800-730-2215;
57 Adapted from Statistics Canada, "Imports, exports and trade balance of goods on a balance-of-payments basis, by country or country grouping," http://www40.statcan.ca/l01/cst01/gblec02a.htm. Statistics Canada information is used with the permission of Statistics Canada. Users are forbidden to copy this material and/or disseminate the data, in an original or modified form, for commercial purposes, without the expressed permission of Statistics Canada. Information on the availability of the wide range of data from Statistics Canada can be obtained from Statistics Canada's Regional Offices, its World Wide Web site at http://www.stats.can.ca, and its toll-free access number 1-800-263-1136.

Chapter 5

76 Adapted from "Jidoka and Autonomation: A Pillar of the Toyota Production System," (Strategos, Inc.), http://www.strategosinc.com/jidoka.htm. Reprinted with permission from Strategos, Inc.

Chapter 6

84 Adapted from *The World of Business: A Canadian Profile*, Student Workbook 4th Ed. by Murphy/Wilson/Notman. 2002. Reprinted with permission of Nelson, a division of Thomson Learning: www.thomsonrights.com. Fax: 1-800-730-2215;
92 Copyright 2007 by ACT, Inc. All rights reserved. Available at http://www.act.org/workkeys/case/bradner.html. Adapted for this use with permission. No further reproduction is permitted without additional specific permission.

Chapter 8

118 Adapted from *The World of Business*, Student Workbook 3rd Ed. by Kelly. 1995. Reprinted with permission of Nelson, a division of Thomson Learning: www.thomsonrights.com. Fax: 1-800-730-2215; **132** Adapted from "Fast-food biz wants K-Fed ad spiked" by Basem Boshra (National Post), January 25, 2007. Material reprinted with the express permission of: "National Post Company," a CanWest Partnership.

Chapter 9

138 Adapted from *The World of Business: A Canadian Profile*, Student Workbook 4th Ed. by Murphy/Wilson/Notman. 2002. Reprinted with permission of Nelson, a division of Thomson Learning: www.thomsonrights.com. Fax: 1-800-730-2215.

Chapter 10

153 From *The World of Business: A Canadian Profile*, Student Workbook 4th Ed. by Murphy/Wilson/Notman. 2002. Reprinted with permission of Nelson, a division of Thomson Learning: www.thomsonrights.com. Fax: 1-800-730-2215; **161** Adapted from "Faith Seekers" by Roger Pierce, http://www.enterprisetoronto.com/index.cfm?linkid=99&linktype=mainlink&content_id=1399&fromurl=keytopics&keyTopicid=48. 2005. Reprinted with permission from the author.

Chapter 11

173 Adapted from "Remembering the MCM/70" by Rachell Ross (Toronto Star), September 25, 2003. Reprinted with permission from The Toronto Star.

Chapter 12

178 From *The World of Business*, Student Workbook 3rd Ed. by Kelly. 1995. Reprinted with permission of Nelson, a division of Thomson Learning: www.thomsonrights.com. Fax: 1-800-730-2215; **184** Adapted from *The World of Business: A Canadian Profile*, Student Workbook 4th Ed. by Murphy/Wilson/Notman. 2002. Reprinted with permission of Nelson, a division of Thomson Learning: www.thomsonrights.com. Fax: 1-800-730-2215.

Chapter 13

196 Adapted from Canadian Bankers Association, www.cba.ca, http://www.cba.ca/en/content/stats/DB251%20-%202006%20-%20eng%20updated%20NO%20Formula(2).pdf. Page 8. Reprinted with permission; **205** Adapted from *The World of Business*, Student Workbook 3rd Ed. by Kelly. 1995. Reprinted with permission of Nelson, a division of Thomson Learning: www.thomsonrights.com. Fax: 1-800-730-2215; **207** Adapted from Canadian Bankers Association, www.cba.ca, http://www.cba.ca/en/content/stats/delivery%20channels%202005_eng.pdf. Reprinted with permission; **212** Adapted from Canadian Bankers Association, www.cba.ca, http://www.cba.ca/en/content/reports/2004%20Technology%20Attitudes.pdf. Reprinted with permission.

Chapter 14

217 Table data © Copyright Tim Carter/AsktheBuilder.com. Reprinted with permission; **228** Adapted from *The World of Business*, Student Workbook 3rd Ed. by Kelly. 1995. Reprinted with permission of Nelson, a division of Thomson Learning: www.thomsonrights.com. Fax: 1-800-730-2215; **230** Adapted from http://www.investopedia.com/articles/basics/06/contemplatingcollectibles.asp, by Andrew Beattie, August 18, 2006. Reprinted with permission from Investopedia.com.

Chapter 15

240 Adapted from *The World of Business*, Student Workbook 3rd Ed. by Kelly. 1995. Reprinted with permission of Nelson, a division of Thomson Learning: www.thomsonrights.com. Fax: 1-800-730-2215; **243** Adapted from *The World of Business: A Canadian Profile*, Student Workbook 4th Ed. by Murphy/Wilson/Notman. 2002. Reprinted with permission of Nelson, a division of Thomson Learning: www.thomsonrights.com. Fax: 1-800-730-2215; **246** Adapted from *The World of Business: A Canadian Profile*, Student Workbook 4th Ed. by Murphy/Wilson/Notman. 2002. Reprinted with permission of Nelson, a division of Thomson Learning: www.thomsonrights.com. Fax: 1-800-730-2215; **247** Adapted from "Credit cards - convenience at a price" by Tom McFeat (CBC News Online). September 20, 2004. http://www.cbc.ca/news/background/personalfinance/creditcards.html. Reprinted with permission from CBC News Online.